Stories of the

SUPERNATURAL

Stories of the

SUPERNATURAL

Finding **GOD**
in Walmart and
Other Unlikely Places

TYLER JOHNSON

DESTINY IMAGE® PUBLISHERS, INC.
P.O. Box 310, Shippensburg, PA 17257-0310

"Speaking to the Purposes of God for This Generation and for the Generations to Come."

Some photos were taken by: Jonathan Taylor, photographer
www.jonathanswriting.com

This book and all other Destiny Image, Revival Press, MercyPlace, Fresh Bread, Destiny Image Fiction, and Treasure House books are available at Christian bookstores and distributors worldwide.

For a U.S. bookstore nearest you, call 1-800-722-6774.
For more information on foreign distributors, call 717-532-3040.
Or reach us on the Internet: www.destinyimage.com

ISBN 10: 0-7684-3164-6
ISBN 13: 978-0-7684-3164-3

For Worldwide Distribution, Printed in the U.S.A.

1 2 3 4 5 6 7 8 9 10 11 / 14 13 12 11 10

Dedication

This book is for the precious Holy Spirit.

God in us,
God with us,
God, my Friend.

Acknowledgments

Thank you to all who have encouraged me to live by the Spirit rather than by the natural laws of this world. You have taught me that a gospel that lacks the miraculous is not the Gospel because the Bible never presented anything less.

Bill Johnson, your humility and steadfastness in pursuing and teaching the supernatural has given me much life. Thank you.

Heidi Baker, your abandoned life of intimacy as well as preaching the Gospel to the poor with signs and wonders following has shown me the balance of the first and second commandment that I yearn to faithfully walk in. You are beautiful, my sister.

David Hogan, your stories have validated the cry in my heart for a Gospel that works. You have shown me what it means to be the answer for those who are in desperate need, and the compassion you walk in is akin to Jesus. Thank you for giving it all and for resisting any form of hypocrisy.

Mike Bickle, your teachings on Song of Songs, fasting, and prayer have revolutionized my life, and the miracles in this book are the result. Thank you.

Christine, thank you for the extravagant love you give to the Bridegroom and to me every day. You are the love of my life and the fulfillment

of my dreams for a wife and mother. Life would not be life without you. Thank you for your encouraging notes as you laboriously edited this book. You are my delight!

Adam Short, you are a wonderful man of God and my best friend. I would be filled with desire for Jesus far less if you were not in my life. I look forward to years of learning from you and drawing from the well of wisdom and passion that God has put in you. You are priceless.

Jonathan, thank you for your laughter and love. Your desire to see the Church come into its creative potential will result in many coming to revelation of Jesus' true nature. Thank you for your contribution to this book by showing me the beauty found in words on a page. Jess, you are like a lost sister we finally found.

Marc and Lydia, you are my friends, parents, fellow ministers, and heroes. Without you this book would not exist. The purity of spirit that you possess astounds me. You have affirmed the yearnings of my heart for intimacy with Jesus and His power, have been relentlessly loyal in relationship with me, and don't just talk about Kingdom living but live it. I look forward to the Day when forerunners are given the honor they are due, for you will find yourselves seated amidst humble kings. I love you both.

Endorsements

Stories of the Supernatural: Finding God in Walmart and Other Unlikely Places is a book that will refresh, encourage, and inspire. It is a compilation of stories about extraordinary acts of courage that bring the Kingdom of Heaven to earth—manifest in miracles, signs, and wonders. Each chapter has an amazing story of people encountering God through the simple courage of a believer. These testimonies also bring an instructional element as the author candidly reveals the "how to" behind each story. In reading this book you will be encouraged and challenged to see God invade the lives of those around you.

Bill Johnson
Pastor, Bethel Church
Author of *When Heaven Invades Earth* and *Release the Power of Jesus*

Testimonies are integral to producing overcoming faith, because they are literally the "Word of God" becoming flesh in the life of the believer. The Word must manifest—it must be demonstrated. The writer of Hebrews tells us that true faith always produces tangible substance. The apostle Paul tells us that God's Kingdom is not just talk, it is power (see 1 Cor. 4:20). Tyler's book offers a great compendium of testimonies—God

stories that are not merely the product of faith; they are stories that will inspire faith itself.

John Crowder
Sons of Thunder

Stories of the Supernatural will stir your faith as you see a beautiful demonstration of what Jesus has commissioned the Church to do. This book truly defines the Church's role that is illustrated in Matthew 10:8. Simply put, we are called to rise up as the Bride of Christ and take dominion over sickness, devils, and death.

When Jesus was asked by the Pharisees in Luke 17:20-21 when the Kingdom of God would come, He replied, "The kingdom of God does not come with your careful observation, nor will people say, 'Here it is,' or 'There it is,' because the kingdom of God is within you." *Stories of the Supernatural* is a wonderful illustration how the Kingdom of God does not come through observation but by demonstration, wrought by the Body of Christ.

Mike Wallace
Kingdom Life International Ministries

Tyler is a man on fire who has caught the vision that God heals and saves today. He is not only pursuing that reality in church settings, but is passionate about God miraculously touching people who are found outside of the church. Tyler's approach to ministry is amazing: By listening to Holy Spirit he tells the Good News to people through demonstrations of power and love. This is the mark of a true evangelist.

Tyler represents a generation that is being raised up by God in this day. This group of people is pushing their way outside the church walls, even outside the revival tents, and onto the streets.

Stories of the Supernatural is an unfolding of what Tyler has witnessed in these least church-like places. It is a simple, sincere, yet powerful account of God's life in one man.

I highly recommend and endorse this book, for it is a modern-day continuation of the book of Acts.

Georgian Banov
Global Celebration

Many people want signs and wonders to take place in their lives and ministries. While this is beneficial, the setting in which a miracle takes place seems to be predominantly limited to a church service. In this book, Tyler shows us that God still wants to reveal Himself to the uninitiated through signs, wonders, and miracles. *Stories of the Supernatural* exhorts us to experience God's Spirit moving in our lives, not confined behind the safety of four walls, but where they are needed most—in the world.

Jim Ford
UK Director, International Fellowship of Ministries

The book *Stories of the Supernatural* will inspire you to release God's supernatural Kingdom to those you meet who need miraculous intervention. You will not only find amazing stories of supernatural encounters, but also insights that will propel you to become a naturally supernatural Christian!

Kevin Dedmon
Pastor, Bethel Church
Author of *The Ultimate Treasure Hunt*

The Body of Christ has a destiny and Kingdom mandate to witness the power of God's love everywhere we go. Tyler Johnson does a great job of sharing testimonies that will encourage believers to step into this destiny.

These stories will show you that you can do it. You can't walk on water sitting in a boat, and these stories should move us to step out of the boat. When we are led by the Holy Spirit, there isn't anything we cannot do.

Cal Pierce
International Director, Healing Rooms Ministries

This book is about hunting for God's treasures: people. Looking for lost treasure is an adventure, especially if you are guaranteed to find something valuable. Through listening prayer and dependence on Holy Spirit we can be guided by God to those He wants to speak to. This book chronicles one man's journey of learning to listen, trust, and care enough to take risks. Maybe you will, too!

Floyd McClung
All Nations

Tyler's book *Stories of the Supernatural* creates a hunger to see the manifest presence of the Lord move through your life. Tyler shares many wild stories of God moving through the lives of believers in daily life situations. This book will release great faith in your heart to see Heaven come to earth.

Jason Phillips
Revival Town Ministries

In Luke 4:18-19 Jesus gave the world at large a quick definition of ministry: *"The Spirit of the Lord is on Me, because He has anointed me to preach good news to the poor. He has sent Me to proclaim freedom for the prisoners and recovery of sight for the blind, to release the oppressed, to proclaim the year of the Lord's favor."* The Spirit and anointing of God has been given to men and women to go and bring change to those who are lost and suffering. Too many times in recent years the anointing and moving of the Holy Spirit have been used primarily as a way of making the Church feel good. While there is nothing wrong with feeling the great

touch of the Spirit on our hearts, Tyler has captured the true essence of the anointing in the life of the believer through this book. To preach, to proclaim, to heal, and to set at liberty is what Jesus was anointed to do.

Through this book, God will stir up within you a desire to step out into realms of faith and trust God for the supernatural in your everyday life. *Stories of the Supernatural* is more than theology; it is a chance to have an encounter with God through the spirit of prophecy as the testimony of Jesus is retold. This is a chance for an awakening on the inside of you as you are encouraged to step out with what you have today.

We are reminded through Tyler's writing that we have all things that pertain to life and godliness within us. You will be blessed to the place of fruitfulness as you read these testimonies. Let the Holy Spirit send you out with your nets ready for the harvest.

Joe Meyering
Pastor and Revivalist, River Glory Church

If you want to be drawn into a new journey into the supernatural, you must read *Stories of the Supernatural.* This book is an invitation for you to join the thousands worldwide whom God is raising up in this hour to transform our planet with His love and power.

The keys in this book are born out of real life experiences. Thus, the stories are raw, real, and genuine. You will be a different person after reading this book as you are empowered to walk in a miraculous lifestyle and to watch impossibilities bow to the name Jesus.

Adam Short
Presence Ministries

The testimony of Jesus is the spirit of prophecy.
(Revelation 19:10)

They overcame him by the blood of the Lamb
and by the word of their testimony…
(Revelation 12:11)

I will open my mouth in parables,
I will utter hidden things…
what we have heard and known…
we will tell the next generation
the praiseworthy deeds of the Lord,
His power, and the wonders He has done.
(Psalm 78:2-4)

Table of Contents

Foreword

"...the testimony of Jesus is the spirit of prophecy."
(Revelation 19:10)

I just finished my second reading of *Stories of the Supernatural* and was wrecked by God's love through it. I found myself crying and confessing to Jesus that I want to fall more in love with Him and walk in the power and Presence of God that this book describes. As I read, I could feel Jesus' sweet Presence as He encouraged me to linger with Him and simply talk. I did so, and He showed me a picture of a homeless man as I lingered with Him.

I had seen this man before, sitting in the parking lot of a grocery store in our town. I have often given money or food to those in need, and have on occasions prayed for their healing. But this time was different. I ended up making my way to the store, spent time loving this man, and witnessed Jesus' Presence overwhelm him. He left with a sparkle in his eye and fresh hope.

Through this book I was led into a vision of someone who needed God's power and love to invade his life. I've heard other stories not unlike the one I just shared from others who have read this book. While reading it, some gave their lives to Jesus, some were healed, and others

who already knew Jesus prior to reading were commissioned to do the work of the ministry mentioned in Matthew 10:8.

In *Stories of the Supernatural,* Tyler demonstrates that as believers we are called to operate in the two greatest commandments. First, we must be overwhelmed by His love, fully experiencing how much God enjoys us and wants to romance His Bride. Only then can we begin to truly fulfill the second command to pour out His love and power on others.

It is not the talents we possess that allow us to receive and release the Kingdom of Heaven on earth today; it is what we *believe.* God isn't necessarily looking for people with credentials, accomplishments, or positions of prestige to shape history. Rather, He chooses the "whosoevers" who desire Jesus' Presence and power described in this book. He is looking for those who are hungry. These are the ones who will change the course of history.

This book demonstrates the reality of how God created each believer to minister the fullness of the Gospel—not a gospel that only consists of words, but a Gospel of power that results in miracles and transformed lives. The stories you read in the pages of this book are real, actual examples of God's love for people demonstrated through someone who is willing to believe God and risk.

"Can anyone do these types of healings, miracles, words of knowledge, signs, and wonders?" you ask. Yes, provided they, like Tyler, lay down their lives to see the true Gospel manifest through developing a lifestyle of intimacy with Jesus. Doing so is costly, but it's a price eagerly paid by those filled with passion and integrity. We are continually inspired and challenged to risk more as we walk alongside this man.

As we come to know and love Holy Spirit while asking big of God, we will see Heaven open up and redeem this natural earthly realm. Tyler exemplifies this type of lifestyle through the stories in this book. As you read, you will be challenged to step out and bring Heaven to earth. You

are called to be a history maker and to set captives free. The moment you accepted Jesus as your Lord and Savior, you were commissioned to do what Jesus did, and even greater works than the miracles wrought by Jesus! (See John 14:12.) If you step out in faith expressed through risk, you will begin to see an increase of miracles in your life. Eventually you will have your own book full of testimonies. Now, go and heal the sick, cleanse the lepers, raise the dead, cast out devils; freely as you have received, freely give (see Matt 10:8).

Marc & Lydia Buchheit
Regional Directors
International Association of Healing Rooms

Preface

This is a book of stories. Each testimony consists of some sort of miraculous event such as a healing, miracle, word of knowledge, or salvation.

Throughout history the world has made use of story in order to teach, pass down values to the emerging generation, give hope, and entertain. It matters not what culture you observe; the consistency of the use of story is unbroken throughout history. Stories are told from every tribe huddled around bonfires in remote settings to every developed and prosperous nation as witnessed through the movie industry. The world revolves around the use of story.

More importantly, God constantly reminds His people throughout Scripture to remember the works of the Lord. I have learned that if I don't write down things God has done I will forget them within a few years. Because of the power of encouragement that is found in remembrance, I started writing down acts of God that I witnessed. When my faith was struggling I would reread the stories of what God had done and I would immediately experience hope and the replenishing of my faith. God had His people stack up memorial stones because He knew what trials lay before them, and He wanted them to have a reservoir of encouragement

stored up for when the trials struck (see Josh. 4:1-9). The use of remembrance will pull you out of the mire.

Also, recounting moments when Jesus did something fantastic releases a spirit of prophecy. Revelation 19:10 says, "...the testimony of Jesus is the spirit of prophecy." Because of its creative nature, the spirit of prophecy enables the recounted miracle to happen in the lives of the hearers. Telling stories of what Jesus has done plants a seed for that very miracle to sprout forth again. Testimony is not only declaring what God has done, but what He will do.

Lastly, Scripture tells us that the Church will ultimately overcome the enemy through two primary means: by the blood of Jesus and by the power of testimony (see Rev. 12:11). The use of testimony is imperative if a person is going to live victoriously. Being grounded in the things that God has done will lead a person into living as more than a conqueror. God wants us to think and live as revivalists rather than survivalists. This is one reason why God constantly reminded His people in Scripture to remember the works of the Lord.

I wrote this book as a way for me to not forget what He has done in my life. In no way was this book like a belt that I kept my notches counted on, but rather, it is a list of times that God used an imperfect person to bring His perfect Kingdom to someone's life.

This book will encourage you in your faith and will exhort you to be used by God to minister supernaturally. You will be challenged, built up in your faith, and filled with desire for more of Jesus.

—Tyler Johnson
November 3, 2008

Healings

But He was pierced for our transgressions,
He was crushed for our iniquities;
the punishment that brought us peace was upon Him,
and by His wounds we are healed.
(Isaiah 53:5)

…those who believe…will place their hands on sick people,
and they will get well.
(Mark 16:17-18)

The Dance of Joy

Several years ago, my friends and I traveled to Mongolia in hopes that within her borders we would find the mystery and wonder that our hearts searched for. Our leader sent us to a group of people who lived deep in the woods, 100 miles from the nearest town. They had come to know Jesus two weeks prior to our visit, and our leader felt that God wanted to do some physical healing with them. After a long journey, we got out of our van and started to ask the group of new converts for people who needed physical healing. I was totally unaccustomed to the power of God, but regardless, I began to look for people who needed prayer.

A man took me by the hand and led me through the group of new believers to an elderly woman who was hidden in the back. Her body was twisted by rheumatoid arthritis. Her arms were of little use to her and she could barely walk. Running was an impossibility. She was 74 years old

and the hobble that she had as she approached me revealed that the arthritis had been with her for years. She slowly brought her two crumpled hands together the best she could, motioning for me to pray. She wanted to be rid of the extraordinary pain that plagued her joints. I looked this woman in the eyes and all I could see was raw need and expectation.

I didn't know how to pray. I had never seen someone get healed before. I didn't want to be like the majority of ministers I saw on television. I didn't want hype. I wanted real.

In one moment, three truths suddenly became unavoidably clear to me.

First, I realized that Jesus healed every person who ever asked Him for healing. He never told one person that it wasn't His will to heal them. Though for the previous 22 years of my life it had been a question that haunted me in every situation, from that point on I no longer wondered if it was God's will or not to heal a person.

Second, I realized that if Jesus were standing next to that woman at that moment, He would heal her. He always healed anyone who asked Him in the Gospels, so He would now. He is the same yesterday, today, and forever (see Heb. 13:8).

Third, I realized Jesus was in *me*, so He *was* standing next to that woman.

I prayed the simplest prayer. I said, "Jesus, heal this woman." Nothing happened. So I prayed again, saying the same thing. This time she was healed. She was so instantly healed by the power and love of God that she took off running in a dead sprint across the field where we stood.

We couldn't speak the same language, but we sure could laugh the same language. We danced out in the field laughing at the wonder and beauty of God. And I will never forget it.

The Now Eggless Red-Light District

A few days after I had the honor of seeing Jesus touch the woman with rheumatoid arthritis, my friend Jonathan and I made our way to the downtown area of Mongolia's capital city, Ulaanbaatar. We began looking on the streets for two girls we had introduced to Jesus a few weeks prior.

Being the only ones in the family who could work, the two girls spent every night on the street in the red-light district selling hard-boiled eggs in order to make ends meet for their family. Their dad had left the family early on, and the mother couldn't work because she was so ill. When on the street, these two little girls were taken advantage of regularly by men who were drunk. Their precious earnings and bodies were stolen from, but the girls courageously paid the cost to meet the family's monetary need.

We had been given extra money for this trip and hoped to give it away to someone in need. Jonathan's heart was burdened for these two girls to be educated. Because a year's worth of income in Ulaanbaatar was a measly $200, he decided that it would be an appropriate amount to give to the family so that both girls could get off the street and attend school for a year. The money would drastically change their lives. We planned to give it indirectly to the family through a local missionary, but first we wanted to meet their mother and see where they lived.

After a few moments of looking for the girls in the red-light district, Jonathan spotted one of the sisters. We had a short conversation with her through a translator, then asked her if she would take us to her house. She agreed, and we jammed into a small, overcrowded taxi that made its way out of downtown Ulaanbaatar and into a dimly lit neighborhood on the outskirts of town. As we stepped out of the taxi and onto a dirt road, we noticed that we had entered a very poor neighborhood. Most of the houses were not much more than shacks. We followed our little friend as she skipped over large mud puddles and trash.

When we arrived at their little home, we met their mother, who wasn't at all excited that we had come into her home uninvited. She was bedridden, and looked as though she was pregnant, despite her age. The disease had taken advantage of her body so badly that most of her organs had swollen to at least double their size, and her stomach was visible proof. In addition, her joints caused her so much pain that struggling her way to the toilet during the day robbed her of the little energy that she had. I couldn't imagine her living very long in that state.

As we talked with the daughter and irritated mother, an idea began to take shape in my mind. Why not pray for the mother to be healed?

We sat down at her bed, and within moments she was born again, obviously quite white for harvest. Next, we prayed for her healing. As we prayed, healing and peace came over her, and she fell fast asleep.

The next day the woman woke up to find her stomach not swollen with sickness, but flat. Her joints were completely pain free, and her energy level was sky high. She felt so good that she went outside and started planting a garden as she thanked Jesus for what He had done. Later on that week she went out and got a job, and the girls were able to stop selling eggs at night in the red-light district of the city. On top of that, the mother soon started a ministry out of the back of her house, taking care of others who were less fortunate than herself.

A family was completely transformed by the result of one healing.

A Risk of Injury to Obey

I was living in Kansas City and my friends and I were having church at home rather than going to a traditional church service for fellowship. Our group was small, but tightly knit in love. We would eat, then go into the living room and worship and pray together. God would show up in various ways.

I remember one night when His Love filled the room to a remarkable degree. Everyone just sat there awestruck, not saying a thing. One dear friend of ours started shaking uncontrollably because Love came into the room so intensely. The shaking was caused by areas of darkness in her life and was not a manifestation of the Holy Spirit. The Presence of God was forcing demons in her life to reveal themselves, though they desired to stay hidden. We prayed over her and she became free. She was a completely different person after she experienced deliverance. If you want to

get healthy, get into His Presence. It will make the impurities rise to the surface.

One other evening, a few of us were preparing dinner for our time of fellowship. The front door opened and our friend HanMarie came into the house. She wasn't walking but was being carried by others. She shared that earlier that day she had injured her lower back so badly that she couldn't walk on her own anymore. The pain was overwhelming.

We ate dinner and then went into the living room to pray as we normally did. HanMarie was in tears, so we decided to pray for her healing. She lay down on her stomach and we placed our hands on her back.

As we prayed various prayers, I was reminded of the level of obedience to the Voice that healers of old walked in. Smith Wigglesworth would do anything that God told him to do, even hit people. The odd thing is that the people were always healed when he would do something that would normally inflict pain upon someone. Smith walked in faith so deeply that natural laws continually bowed in surrender to Jesus in him.

One time Wigglesworth punched a man with stomach cancer directly in the area that was overrun by disease. Because the man was bedridden, he came to the healing meeting in a stretcher. The man was so close to death that his doctor was required to escort him to the gathering. When Smith punched the guy, he flatlined. The doctor told Smith that he was going to have him arrested for killing his patient. But God had told Smith to do it, so he stuck to his guns and just kept moving down the prayer line, unphased. In fact, Smith turned around as he was walking away from the doctor and told him, "He is healed." Obviously not, Smith—the guy was dead. But faith sees that which is not yet a reality as a present reality (see Heb. 11:1). Two minutes later the man jumped up from his stretcher, raised from the dead *and* totally healed.

Another time, Smith kicked a child who was completely crippled off the stage that he was standing on. He booted the child like a football, and it is said that the little boy hit the ground running, entirely restored.

If that doesn't try your assumptions about how God works, I don't know what would. That level of obedience makes me uncomfortable to say the least, but you have to judge a tree by its fruit. The reality is that Smith saw people healed whom others had prayed for and given up on.

Obviously, you have to know you are hearing from God when you move in obedience at such an extreme level. While we were praying, the Lord told me to find the place in HanMarie's back that hurt the most, and then press on it, hard. He told me that if I didn't press on it hard, she wouldn't be healed. He wanted to see if I would put obeying Him over preserving a relationship with a good friend. He wanted to see if I was more filled with the fear of man or the fear of God.

So I pressed on it hard. A minute later, my dear friend Johanda grabbed HanMarie's hands and raised her to her feet. As HanMarie stood to her feet and moved, she realized that the pain she had been experiencing was suddenly absent.

Joy overtook us. We cranked up worship music, and HanMarie burst through the front door and ran into the front yard, when five minutes before she couldn't even walk. She started dancing before the Lord, bending her body in all sorts of beautiful ways. She was healed!

The rest of us joined her in the front yard, dancing and singing before the Lord with worship music blaring. The neighbors must have thought we had lost our minds.

The Faith of a Child

My friend Christine and I, along with my two nephews, Jamin and Jonah, decided to go to Walmart to pray for the sick. Jonah was 4 years old. Jamin was 6.

We parked in the lot outside the store and waited on the Lord for a brief amount of time. We got some pictures of people God wanted to touch, broke up into two groups, and hopped out of the car. Jamin and I were a team, and Christine and Jonah were a team.

The first picture that Jamin and I had written down was of a material with blue and white horizontal stripes. We didn't know what problem the person wearing the stripes had with his or her body, but we decided that God would show us when we found him or her.

We walked around the store a few times looking for this mystery person. Jamin's eyes were peeled like an eagle circling a lake, looking for

that perfect fish to nab. I loved watching him anticipate and expect God to move in miraculous ways.

Then suddenly, there it was: the blue and white striped shirt. The owner of the blue and white stripes was a girl not much older than 16 years. She was standing in line, paying for the items she had picked out. Jamin's keen eyes picked her out from quite a distance, and we started walking toward this stranger, not knowing what we would say when we got there.

Once we were standing next to her, we asked her if there was anything wrong with her body, because God had highlighted her to us and we believed that He wanted to heal whatever was wrong with her body.

At that point I realized that the woman standing next to her was her mother because the girl looked at her with wide eyes and said, "Oh my gosh, that is crazy. I was just telling my mom that my shoulder and my elbow have started hurting a lot these last few days. We were just talking about what we should do, and thinking that I need to get it checked out by a doctor."

The moment she said that, a guy walked over and stood behind her. It was her brother. Now we didn't have just one girl, but a whole family would be able to see God show off. I asked her if we could pray healing over her, and she agreed.

In the middle of the checkout aisles, with people buzzing past and around us, I lifted Jamin up into my arms so that he could reach this girl's shoulder and elbow. I wanted Jamin to be the one praying, for many reasons. Children can effect miracles better than adults. Jesus said the Kingdom belongs to those such as children (see Matt. 19:14). Kids are a gateway into the miraculous realm. They believe. Life is simple to a child. They know God is good, and as a result they know that He wants people to be well. Also, they are not threatening to a stranger. Very few people

are going to turn a kid down when the child asks if he or she can pray for the adult.

Jamin gently laid his little hands on this girl's shoulder and prayed the most beautiful, faith-filled prayer; "Jesus, heal this shoulder. We know You love people. Make her shoulder better."

Jamin's prayer caused the atmosphere around us to shift. I could feel Heaven fill the space around us, as if the air became thicker in the most delightful of ways. I felt the pleasures that God's presence brings, and it made me pleasantly lightheaded.

I set Jamin back down on his feet and I asked the girl to try to do something with her shoulder that would have caused her pain before. She started moving her shoulder, and an overwhelmingly large smile stretched across her face. She looked at her mom and said, "It doesn't hurt! I can't believe it. It was hurting just a few minutes ago!"

Next I asked her how her elbow was doing. She tried it out and said that it still hurt. I picked Jamin up again; he laid his hands on her elbow, and prayed again. She started moving her arm so that her elbow was exercised, and the smile that had spread itself before was visible again.

We stood back and said, "Jesus did this to show you that He loves you." Then we walked off and left them in their stupor.

I looked down at Jamin. He was already scoping the store for his next victim. I said, "Jamin! God just used you to heal someone!" He simply said, "Yeah" and kept walking, looking around the store. I didn't understand Jamin's demeanor and reaction to what had just happened. Did he not understand what had just taken place at his fingertips? Was he overwhelmed, or worse, did he think he was the one who made the miracle happen? I couldn't discern what he was feeling or thinking.

Then it hit me: Jamin wasn't *surprised* that God had healed someone through him. He wasn't lacking excitement or awe, only surprise. It

was as if by his confident strut he was saying, "Why not? If God is really God, and He is my God, then why wouldn't people be healed when I lay hands on them and pray?" Jamin wasn't gloating in himself; he was confidently boasting in God.

Most people go through their entire lives and never see one miracle take place before their eyes when they lay hands on people, but Jamin saw it happen when he was only 6. He believed God was good and had the faith of a child. The Kingdom belongs to such as these...

Smoke Fills the Temple

I have noticed that before I ever became conscious of the Holy Spirit, I would nonetheless interact with Him without knowing it. For example, when I was first saved I would find myself inhaling deeply throughout my day, and I had no idea why. All I knew was that after I did it, I just felt full of God. It wasn't the regular breathing of air...it was as if I was taking something into my body that was life-giving yet invisible. I never quite understood the logic behind it.

I have a video of myself preaching shortly after I got saved. It is humorous how you can see me pause between sentences at points, inhale a few times, then continue speaking.

At the time I didn't put two and two together and realize that every time I inhaled, the Spirit of God would fill me. Though at the time I didn't have much scriptural backing for what was happening, it worked for me nonetheless.

For a number of years I have had the privilege of ministering in the Healing Rooms, where we pray for the sick and those who are hungry for more of God. One night, a man came in for prayer who had emphysema. He and his wife had come to know Jesus just a week before, and their hearts were incredibly pliable. They were hungry for more of God and believed that God was the answer to all of their addictions, lack of finances, and physical problems. The emphysema was a result of all the smoking the man had done.

The couple was quite unrefined, hadn't ever been in a religious setting before, and possessed a wonderful level of expectancy toward God that He would move on their behalf. Their lack of religious thinking kept a box from being created around God and naturally invited Him to work in any way He found fit, even if it was controversial.

Religious people put God in a box so that they feel like they understand Him and how He works. It is an issue rooted in control, which boils down to fear, and fear is sin.

But this couple was nothing like that; they didn't care how their answers came—they just wanted things to be made well. They didn't have a box. They didn't have an agenda as to how God could and couldn't work. As a result, their hearts were receptive and moldable in the most beautiful way.

As we were praying for this man, I got a strong impression that holy smoke was in the room. I had never heard of that before. I felt like the Lord was telling me that this man simply needed to breathe in this smoke and he would be healed.

I was standing behind him, so I made my way around to the front of him and I grabbed his hands to pray. I looked down at his chest and was surprised to see that on the front of his shirt it simply said, "Breathe." That was confirmation enough for me. I told him to breathe in God's

Presence and his lungs would be healed. He took a few short breaths, wheezing and all. I said, "No, I mean big breaths. Come on, inhale in faith!" He started to breathe in and out, very deeply and slowly. He coughed a few times, then continued to breathe deeply, over and over again. After about a minute his wheezing went away. He looked at us and said, "Well, it feels better, that is for sure." We prayed and prophesied over him for a while, then he left and another person entered the room for prayer.

The next week I saw the man and his wife excitedly sitting in the waiting room of the Healing Rooms, wanting more prayer. We brought them into the prayer room and asked them how they were doing. The man looked at us and said, "My lungs are healed! I have been able to breathe fine for the last week. I woke up the morning after you guys prayed for me, and I could breathe perfectly!" I listened to him breathe deeply and sure enough, the heavy wheezing that he had one week before was gone.

I started to seek God on this bizarre reality of holy smoke. Surprisingly, holy smoke is mentioned in Isaiah 6 and Revelation 15. It started to become clear to me that the smoke of this world is a counterfeit of the smoke that is conceived by the Presence of God. Because the enemy does not have the ability to create, his only option is to distort and twist the things that God has created. The smoke of this world harms our bodies, but holy smoke heals our bodies. Likewise, while drug use opens a gateway to the demonic realm, the holy smoke of Heaven opens a gateway to heavenly realms. If we inhale the smoke of Heaven while in prayer, we can visit heavenly realms with ease.

After all, we are God's temple. Isaiah 6:4 tells us that the temple was filled with smoke when God showed up. The temple needs to be filled, so inhale His Presence. The Holy Spirit is in you, but He is also all around you. Take Him in deeply and reap the benefits of being filled with God.

Three for the Price of One

I was at a conference. The speaker had people with arthritis raise their hands so that those in the crowd around them could lay their hands on them and pray for healing.

Something must have happened, because every person I put my hands on got healed. Three people were healed, one after another. One woman had an arthritic toe that kept her from dancing before the Lord. God hates it when something keeps us from worshiping Him in total freedom. A guy couldn't raise his hands above his head because of the pain in his shoulders. He was healed. Lastly, a woman couldn't bend her knee without extreme pain, which left her also unable to dance in worship. She started laughing and crying as the Lord healed her. When the worship music started up again, it was amazing to watch joy radiate from her as she danced.

We have to pray for the sick and believe that God will heal them. The prayer offered in faith will change circumstances. At the same time, we should pray for anyone and everyone we can even if we don't "feel" faith, because God doesn't even need our feeling faith to do it, just our partnership. We are richly rewarded when we do.

Seek and Find

After training a large group of people on how to hear God's voice and then reach out to those that don't know Him, we split into smaller groups and headed out onto the streets of Spokane, Washington. Through prophetic evangelism our group invaded bars, infiltrated shops, flooded the streets, and saw people saved and healed.

During prayer with my group I had seen a picture of a red shirt and knew that the owner of the shirt suffered from migraines. Another woman in my group had seen a red shirt in prayer as well, which acted as a confirmation that we had been hearing from God.

After walking around downtown and praying with a few people, we stumbled upon a girl wearing a red shirt. We asked her if she suffered from migraine headaches. She smiled and said that she did suffer from migraines, and even had one until the moment we approached her. The

moment we had walked up she was healed of the migraine. The Presence of God healed her on the spot, without us even praying for her. It was what I like to call a "Presence healing."

She didn't know Jesus. She had taken off work so she could eat, thinking that it might help her headache. But she hadn't started eating yet. Then I saw the word "apartment." It turns out she was in the middle of a decision about if she should buy a house or rent another apartment, because her lease was up. We prayed with her about her situation, and went on our way.

You carry the Presence of God in a tremendous way. He is alive in you, and radiates from you in such a fashion that would blind your eyes if you could see its reality. The more we believe that He is *big* in us, the more we will see atmospheres around us shift, which will effortlessly result in healings, miracles, signs, and wonders. God is much bigger in you than anything else is outside you. What is inside your heart and possessing your spirit has more power than any atom bomb that was ever created. Victory lives within you. Start to believe for the dead to be raised in morgues when you simple *drive by* your local funeral home. Why not? It is we that are small, not Him. Start to believe that He is big on the inside, then let Him out.

Spirit Adventures

I once heard about a minister who had an amazing experience while holding a crusade in Uganda.

A witch doctor was hindering the crusade by commanding the clouds to rain day after day. The rain caused thousands of people to flee for shelter under nearby trees and buildings instead of staying in the crusade field where they could hear the Gospel message being preached over the speaker system. Many local Christians begged the evangelist to not challenge this man because he had such a reputation of being able to kill anyone who crossed him with witchcraft. There was no man who was more powerful in witchcraft in the whole country, and he was nationally known.

Becoming increasingly frustrated, the evangelist sought God as to what to do. The Lord told him to continue on as planned and not concern himself about the witch doctor. The Lord made it clear that He would take care of the witch doctor.

The next morning as the evangelist drove up to the crusade grounds he noticed that the witch doctor was not in the middle of the field as he had been every day prior, but he was up on the stage. Shocked, the evangelist wondered how the witch doctor duped his entire staff into allowing this man up on the platform. In disbelief of what he was witnessing, he started asking the pastors around him, "What is the witch doctor doing up on the stage?" The pastors sheepishly told the evangelist to ask the witch doctor himself. The pastors looked scared, or at best embarrassed.

At that very moment, the witch doctor spotted the evangelist and instantly started making his way toward him. With the evangelist boldly standing his ground, the witch doctor briskly walked directly up to the minister and with his face only inches away from the man of God said, "You were in my room last night."

Confused, the evangelist assured the witch doctor that he was in his own hotel room the night before, getting some much-needed sleep. The witch doctor persisted, "No, you were in my room last night." The evangelist was unable to deter the witch doctor from believing that he had broken into his home and come into his bedroom, despite the logical arguments he gave. No amount of persuading was going to change the witch doctor's mind. Finally, the witch doctor said, "You don't understand. I realize you were asleep in your hotel room last night. I believe you. But you came into my room last night, woke me up, and told me about Jesus. You led me to give my life to Him and make Him Lord and Savior of my life. I serve Jesus now, and have turned my back on witchcraft." Though he was asleep, God took the evangelist's spirit and manifested it in the natural realm so as to bring the witch doctor to salvation.

The former witch doctor then took the microphone and declared to the entire assembly of people present that the evangelist's God was greater than the spirits he had previously served. He had been waiting on the stage because he was so excited to tell the evangelist about what had happened to him. Many people gave their lives to Jesus as a result of this man's profession about God's power.

It's odd, but it is possible for our spirit to go on adventures as we sleep. God is so incredibly gracious that He will even use us in our sleep to further the Kingdom. This story and what it taught me about translation was brought to my mind one day because of something that happened to my son.

When our son was 6 months old, he woke up very early one morning with a dangerously high temperature. We prayed for him, gave him different kinds of fever-reducing medicines, and took baths with him. But despite everything we tried, his temperature continued to rise. I began fasting. Every time we packed up to go to the hospital, his temperature would briefly plummet. Once we canceled the trip his temperature would spike up higher than before. We didn't know what to do besides resist fear and continue to believe that God would move on our behalf.

It is one thing to believe God for other people's healings, but what you believe is thoroughly tested when disease comes to your own family. Your Gospel must work inside *and* outside the home. We decided to stand in faith, though fear was tearing at the door of our hearts persisting for entrance.

Out of sheer exhaustion from getting up so early and the constant maintenance required in caring for a sick baby, Christine and I, along with our son, took a nap. As we slept, I had a dream that my wife and I were sitting on the front row in a small church as a powerful man of God named David Hogan preached. Toward the end of his sermon he asked, "How many of you were translated in the spirit to attend this meeting?"

Though in the dream I was sure I came by car, my arm involuntarily shot up. He looked at us and acknowledged our presence. Then I woke up.

The moment I awoke, God clearly told me to have Christine and I lay our hands on Joshua again, praying for his healing. We did so, and his temperature returned to normal. It did not rise again, and he was healed.

I thought about what had happened for quite some time. It occurred to me that while Christine and I did not have the anointing to break this fever, David Hogan did. In the midst of our lack, God is gracious. He literally sent us to David Hogan so that the anointing that is on him could get on us. Though we were asleep, God took our spirits where David was ministering in that particular hour in the natural realm. The Lord physically manifested our spirits in real life so that we could get what we needed in order for our son to recover.

Odd or not, it worked. I don't know how a prophet's bones raised the dead either, but it is in the Bible (see 2 Kings 13:20-21). So is the time Phillip was taken away from the Ethiopian eunuch by the Spirit and suddenly appeared in Azotus (see Acts 8:39-40).

Words of Knowledge

To one is given…through the Spirit…the word of knowledge
(1 Corinthians 12:8 NKJV)

A secular explanation of the word of knowledge
on Wikipedia.org:

"What separates words of knowledge from other times of immanence is that most words of knowledge are delivered in times where a person is going about their everyday life. A common example might be as follows: a man is walking down the street, walks up to a woman he has never met, and names a problem in her life, such as psychological problems, secret addictions, recent deaths, or illness. Unlike information delivered by a contemporary prophet or historical fortunetellers such as Nostradamus or Ms. Cleo, most words of knowledge contain precise detail, such as a name, the part of the body that is sick, or a problem few people know about. Thus, the opportunity for coincidence is virtually eliminated. The person who is approached is often left scared and frightened, because a person she has never met has just approached her, told intimate details about her life, and left as quickly as he came. However, the purpose of the Holy Spirit passing on a word of knowledge is never to make a person afraid (other than Godly fear leading to salvation) but to help them deal with an issue in their life, such as unforgiveness for example. For this reason words of knowledge are often followed by prayer or talking through the issue or action relevant to the word of knowledge such as the receiver of the word of knowledge forgiving someone."

A Mother's Concern

I was desperate to see God do the things I read about in the Bible, so I started praying for at least one person every day for healing. I decided that he or she had to be a stranger whom I had never met before.

After a week I realized that healing and the prophetic don't do very well without each other. The percentage of people who are healed decreases dramatically when these two tools are used separately. I came to realize that the prophetic helps direct how to pray and for whom to pray when you are looking for people to touch with God's healing. In addition, if the two are joined together in one unified flow of the Spirit, the person never walks away empty handed, because even if he (or she) doesn't get instantly healed, you will still deliver a word that touches his heart.

One day I was driving to Walmart and I asked the Lord for a prophetic word. I saw a picture of some clothing that was woven and gray. I asked the Lord what I should pray for when I found the person wearing

the gray woven clothing. He gave me a picture of a mother holding the hand of a young boy, and the boy was being pulled away from the mom.

I arrived at Walmart, went inside, and started walking around looking for someone wearing this type of material. I finally found a woman wearing a sweatshirt that was gray, and the material looked woven. She happened to be a Walmart employee. After a few moments of getting some boldness and faith from God, I approached her.

I asked her if she knew where the webcams were, even though I knew where they were. I wanted to get her in a place where we wouldn't be interrupted. When we got to the webcams, I asked her if she had a young boy. She said yes, and was shocked that I knew that. I asked, "Is he about this tall?" as I held my hand above the floor at about the height I saw in the vision. She said yes. I told her about the picture that I saw as I was on my way to Walmart, and she "tripped out." She said, "Man, that is so crazy. That is so crazy." Then I asked her if she felt like her son was being torn away from her. She said, "Oh my gosh. How did you know that? His dad is in jail, and lately he has been writing my son letters in an attempt to persuade him to abandon me and go live with him once he is out of prison."

She didn't know Jesus, but I said, "Come with me. We are going to pray for your little boy. Your situation is about to change. God wouldn't have told me if it wasn't." We started down the aisles together, praying together as we walked. After the prayers had finished, she looked at me with an astonished face, thanked me, and went back to work.

It was my first word of knowledge at Walmart. Though it was simple, this woman was touched with God's love through supernatural knowledge of her life. A God she didn't know suddenly made Himself known by showing that He knew all about her.

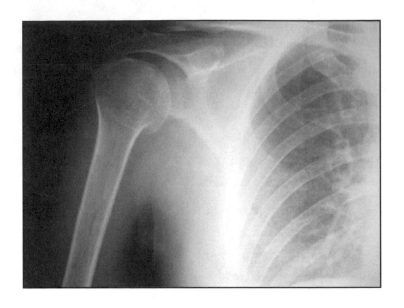

Jacob, Now Israel

Once again, I was at Walmart. While sitting in the car I saw a picture of red flannel, so I assumed that I was to look for someone with a red flannel shirt on. I felt like whoever was wearing the flannel would have a problem with their right knee. I walked the store for quite awhile, but didn't find anyone with a red flannel shirt on.

I kept looking, and after a few minutes I saw a red flannel hung up all by itself, far from the rack where it was supposed to be hung. I wondered if the person I needed to pray for would be standing near it, pick it up, or at least walk by. I waited, and nothing happened. Then I felt the Lord say, "OK, that is all. Thank you for being obedient. I am very pleased with you." I thought, "That was weird," and headed out of the store with the intention of going home.

Though nothing happened, I didn't get bummed, because I do whatever He tells me to do, even if it doesn't make any sense. Obedience and learning to follow the Holy Spirit are my priorities, not results. If I get skilled at the former, the latter will inevitably follow.

On the way home I stopped at Safeway to buy some candy. Right before I walked in, something in me snapped. I was no longer OK with the fact that nobody had encountered God's healing love that night, so I asked the Lord again for another word.

There comes a point in relationship with God where we are so convinced of what God's will and heart is that we will stand up to anyone who opposes it happening, even God Himself. Jacob knew that the only one standing between himself and God's will for his life wasn't the devil, but God. He wrestled with God until God relented and blessed him.

God wants to bless His people, but sometimes God opposes us in things that are completely within His will for our lives to see how badly we want something. If we crumple in desire for what we are asking for when He tests us by standing in our way, it is clear to Him that we aren't ready to receive it yet. He is a Daddy who wants our best. And He knows that if our conviction about His will in a situation was diminished when He slightly opposed us, we couldn't have handled the temptations that come with the blessing that we were asking for. He doesn't want the blessing of what we are asking for to corrupt us, so He waits until we become so adamant about His heart that we are willing to take anything (even Him) by the horns and wrestle it to the ground like a cowboy does with a bull. This may sound arrogant and presumptuous to those who do not understand the reality of friendship we have with God. But to those who know the heart of God to bless us in every way possible but also to protect us, this makes perfect sense. He wants to bless us, but not at the cost of ruining our lives.

Therefore, He waits until we want good things strongly enough that the favor and worship of man that comes from what we ask for pales in comparison to our drive to see His will be manifested on earth. Once we get to that point, we plow right past Him as He stands in our way. He knows that if we want something enough to stand up to Him, we won't be swayed when man stands up to us, intimidates us, worships us, tries to buy us off with money, or offers us positions of prestige.

The violent take it by force (see Matt. 11:12). God desires His Church to become so bold in the will of God and so convinced of His goodness that we point at Him and say, "No! I know what You want in this situation, and I will not relent until I see Your Kingdom come to earth, even if it is You who challenges me!" His reaction to this type of prayer is not anger, but absolute joy because we are demonstrating our confidence in His love toward us. He smiles, stands aside, follows in step behind us in order to support and work with us, and cheers us on. He is such a wonderful Father.

This night at Safeway, I had reached that point of violence in spirit. I was not at peace with the fact that nobody had been touched by the supernatural love of God that night yet. I was not going to go home empty handed, so I stomped my feet on the ground and demanded Heaven to move on my behalf.

Suddenly, I saw a picture of a woman with brown hair. Her hair was straight, and came down to her shoulders. I felt like she had problems with her right shoulder and her neck.

I looked through the store but didn't find anyone. As I sadly approached the cash register, I saw that the woman at my register fit the description. I said, "Excuse me, Terry. Do you by any chance have problems with your right shoulder?" She said yes. I said, "This is another shot in the dark, but do you also have problems with your neck?" She nodded.

I told her I was a minister in town and that I wanted to pray for her healing. I grabbed her hand and prayed for her, released healing upon her, and prayed about Jesus' love for her. When I finished I asked her how her relationship with the Lord was. She said that it was great. She had been a believer for a long time. We talked for a bit, I told her again how much Jesus loves her, then left the store.

Something happened that night. Ever since then, any time I ask God for a word of knowledge, I get one. Violence in spirit brings breakthrough.

A Fire in the Bakery Section

The night after I received the word about the red flannel, I went to Walmart again. I arrived after hitting a dog with my car and praying for its healing. Any chance I get to raise the dead, right?

I went into Walmart with a few pictures that I had seen earlier in the day. I was still a bit shaken up from hitting the dog. The moment I walked in the door, a guy with a red flannel walked out in front of me. I remembered the vision I had the night before of the red flannel with the right knee. In faith I said to myself, *That word never got fulfilled. Maybe God gave it to me for tonight.* I don't want to assume I know how the Lord speaks, so I am open to Him changing my agenda of how to do things. Therefore, I followed this guy and decided to ask.

I said, "Hey bro, I have a question for you." He was older, with scraggily gray hair and dirty pants. He looked like a logger. He said,

"Yeah?" I asked him if he had a problem with his knee. He said that he did. I told him I had been praying in my car and saw a picture of a guy in the store wearing red flannel who had problems with his right knee. He was taken aback. I asked him if I could pray for him. He stuck out his knee and said, "Yeah, go for it!"

We were in the bakery section. I got down on my knees and laid my hands on him. As I did, a prayer came out of my mouth that I did not consider the most sensitive—nor logical—prayer. I just prayed, "Fire! Fire! Fire!" *What does that even mean anyway?* My mind was thinking, *Are you crazy? Why are you praying this? This dude is going to think you have lost your mind! He doesn't know about God's fire!* Nonetheless, my spirit kept using my mouth rather than my head. That's all right; God, possess my spirit. I figure if He wants to do something, I am not going to stop Him.

Suddenly, I could feel literal warmth fill the air around us, despite the air conditioning that was blowing on us from the vents above. It was now noticeably warmer around us. I got up and he said, "Whoa, what did you do to me? My knee feels like it is on fire! It is burning!" I told him, "Don't worry. That is God doing something." He calmed down as I asked him to try to do something with his knee that he couldn't do before. He started bending his knee back and forth and found that there was no pain. He could now move it with full mobility when that had been an impossibility moments before. We both got very excited as we realized that Jesus had just healed him. The only difference between my excitement and his was that his involved swear words of joy and mine didn't.

I continued to walk around the store, extremely excited about what had just happened. I was laughing and jumping up and down like an idiot. I started to walk around the store, looking for another person to blast with Love. After a few circles around the store, I walked down an aisle hoping to find my next divine appointment. I noticed that in the

aisle parallel to mine was the guy I had just prayed for. He had just walked up to a woman he knew and was talking to her. As I peered past the merchandise on the shelves, I heard him say, "You wouldn't believe what just happened to me. This guy walked up to me and told me that he was praying and saw a picture of me wearing red flannel. He told me what was wrong with my body, prayed for me, and my knee was healed! It was amazing!" The woman exclaimed, "That is amazing! He was a messenger of God." They went on and on about it.

I was sitting there eavesdropping and peering through the aisle, acting like a Peeping Tom. I left the store, laughing even harder than before because I had been called a messenger of God.

In reality, there is no difference between the "messenger of God" and anyone else. Any person who decides to believe everything that is in the Book will do the same things. Let me explain.

Most Christians profess that they believe everything in the Bible, and though the Bible contains page after page of supernatural events, most Christians don't live a supernatural lifestyle. That is a fundamental contradiction.

This contradiction was present in my life for many years. During this time of my life when I lived in this unbiblical fashion, something started to be birthed in my heart that said, "If I really believed the whole Bible, then why doesn't my life look like the lives of the people in the Bible? I either don't believe the whole Bible, or God isn't really the God the Bible says He is. God is not a liar, so I must need to change the way that I read the Bible so that I am not left looking like such an oddball compared to everyone else who walked with God in Scripture. Visions? Trances? Healings? Dead raisings? Prophecies? Tongues?

Instead of lowering the Bible to the level of my experience, I decided to allow the Bible to determine what my life should look like and follow

in step. I decided to allow God to show me the unbelief in my life that kept me from experiencing the things that the people in the Bible experienced rather than changing the way that I read the Bible so that I was comfortable. We can interpret responsibility away if we wish to.

God showed me two ways to determine if I really believed the whole Book or not. He wanted to confront the obvious chasm between what my life looked like and what the lives of the people in the Bible looked like. Their lives were filled with the supernatural, while mine was not.

This was the first measuring rod God gave me to determine if I really believed the whole Bible: He told me, "True belief always becomes action."

There is a difference between what we believe and what we think we believe. You can determine what you *actually* believe and what you *think* you believe by observing what you *do*.

For example, if you really believe God is good and wants to heal the sick like you profess, then you will pray for the sick whenever you encounter them. If you don't believe that God heals the sick or wants to heal the sick, then you will rarely find yourself laying hands on the sick. You may pray in your closet for the sick, but that is because that doesn't involve any risk or faith. When you pray in your closet and God doesn't heal the person, it is no skin off your back. Faith can be measured by the amount of loss you will incur if God doesn't come through and aid you in the situation where you are stepping out. Praying in your closet is great, but if that is all you do, be assured that God has more for you if you would believe. You know you are in faith when what you are trying to do will fail miserably without God supernaturally stepping in on your behalf. We should always be in that place of dependence on God. Anything less is less than what the people in the Bible settled for. A boy with a sling against a giant with a sword? That is risk. That is faith.

Once again, your actions reveal your beliefs. Another example: If you really believe that Jesus was raised from the dead like you profess, then you will pray over dead bodies in an attempt to raise them to life in accordance with Jesus' command in Matthew 10:8. If you don't pray for the dead to be raised, your lack of action reveals that you don't really believe that God raises the dead. And if your actions reveal that you don't believe God raises the dead today, then you have a serious problem on your hands. In not trying to raise the dead, you contradict the most fundamental aspect of Christianity. The crux of Christianity is that a Man was raised from the dead. The issue of dead raising makes or breaks the validity of Christianity, as Paul said in First Corinthians 15. And because God is the same yesterday, today, and forever, if He raised Jesus from the dead in the past, He raises the dead today.

Your action, or lack of action, reveals the actual beliefs of your heart. After I got this revelation, I started praying for the dead to be raised whenever I could. I want to obey God.

The second way God revealed to me how much of the Bible I thought I believed but actually didn't was by highlighting the verse Mark 16:17. In this verse, Jesus says that signs and wonders will follow *those who believe*. This means that if signs and wonders aren't happening wherever you go, you don't really believe. Don't be offended. None of us are perfect in faith. Just recognize your need to believe God, and ask Him to help you in your unbelief.

When I read this verse and realized the lack of belief in my life, I was cut deeply. All the years of living a lie before God grieved me deeply, and I made the changes in my life that were needed in order to really start to believe the Bible. I started to *live out* what I professed to believe, and amazingly, signs and wonders started to follow my life.

Back to the story. I was laughing exuberantly on the other side of the aisle because of being called a "messenger of God." I was encouraged

to hear these two people talk in such a way when I wasn't present; it showed me that the guy wasn't putting on a show and that a miracle had actually happened. Sometimes I am concerned that people may feel like they will disappoint me when they tell me the truth if the outcome I am praying for hasn't happened. I get concerned that they may just tell me what they think I want to hear, rather than telling me the truth about what happened when I prayed. If they didn't get healed, I want to know. The truth doesn't frighten me or hurt my faith at all. I will just pray again until something happens. The surprise and awe on the other side of the aisle showed me that this man didn't need a second prayer.

Introduced to Love

God speaks words of knowledge on the basis of desire. If I don't really want them, they don't come. But if I open myself up to that realm, and position my heart and spirit to receive through expectation and excitement, they always come. Though a person can receive words of knowledge in various ways, I primarily get words of knowledge through pictures. The pictures are so brief that I usually wonder if I even saw something. A split second after I see the picture it isn't present anymore, but it is nonetheless seared into my memory, which makes me suspicious that it is God speaking to me.

A great minister of God once said that if you want to get words of knowledge, pay attention to the random thoughts that you have during prayer and ministry. After hearing that, I started interpreting my random thoughts or pictures as possible words of knowledge. Then I would go try

them out to find out if they were words from God or not. If I felt like a stranger's name was "Jack," I would go ask him. I was always surprised when the word would turn out to be correct, though it came in a way that wasn't "sovereign." Random thoughts or pictures don't feel the least bit sovereign. But if we are waiting for open visions before we minister super-naturally, we may never minister. I decided to start taking what God was giving me and make use of it. I didn't want to be the guy who buried his one talent. I wanted to be faithful with what He had given me so that He could entrust me with more.

Everyone hears from God. They just need to realize that they hear from God. Even unbelievers hear from God regularly—they just don't know it is God. That is why we can interpret dreams for unbelievers through the Holy Spirit like Daniel did (see Dan. 2 and 4). God is speaking to everyone on earth in an attempt to make Himself known to them. Once we realize that God speaks to us in ways that are far simpler than we would ever expect from a sovereign God, we can minister and walk as Jesus did. God is our friend and speaks to us as a friend. He speaks simply and constantly.

Once when I was at Walmart sitting in the car until I got a picture, I saw a picture of a woman turned facing away from me. From the angle that I had on her, I could see that her hair was slightly curly and brown, maybe even dreadlocked. I also felt like there was something wrong with her nose. The feeling that it was her nose was soft and quiet, yet I couldn't shake it. I didn't even think it was a word of knowledge, but after a few minutes it was all I could get, so I got out of the car and went in anyway.

It was around 11:00 at night. I thought to myself, *The chances of there being a woman with dreadlocked hair in Walmart who has a nose problem at eleven o'clock at night are less than slim.* But I decided that the Holy Ghost knew what He is doing.

I walked around, not seeing anyone who looked like the woman in the picture. As I prayed, I felt that whomever I was going to see and meet was going to be up near the registers, and that it may save me time to just wait up there. Despite that nudge from the Holy Spirit I continued to walk around the store. I circled the store three times and didn't find any woman with dreadlocked hair. I saw a lot of women with hair close to what I saw in the picture, but not close enough.

After about ten minutes of walking around the store, I made my way toward the registers. Lo and behold, a woman with the hair I saw in the vision walked right out in front of me. I was astonished.

I decided not to hesitate and immediately walked up behind her. As I did, I realized that I was acting out exactly what I had seen in the vision. I was standing behind her, looking at her hair. She turned, and though I couldn't see anything wrong with her nose, I abruptly introduced myself by asking her if her nose didn't work the way that it should.

She looked at me intently for a moment, let out a nervous laugh, and then told me that she was manic-depressive and a meth addict. She added that she got high everyday, regularly got in fights, and as a result her nose had been broken on average once a month for the last year and a half.

I couldn't believe it! What are the chances? Not only was the picture that God gave me accurate, but God got her to share her deepest, darkest struggles with a total stranger in the first ten seconds of us meeting each other. God is OK with skipping the three or more months it takes to build trust in a natural discipling relationship so that the person can be ministered to in the actual struggles that they are caught in. The only way to get on the fast track in discipleship is to take the route of the supernatural.

She asked me how I knew this about her, and I told her that I had been praying and God had told me. I asked her if I could pray for her. She said yes, but in a way that made me feel like she didn't think she was worthy to receive prayer.

I waited for her to pay for her items and then walked her out to the parking lot. Because of how forward I was when I approached her, I clarified that I wasn't hitting on her, but just wanted to pray for her. I explained how God tells me what is wrong with people's bodies and hearts because He wants to heal them in order to reveal His love to them. She nodded in understanding, so I started praying for her and prayed for healing for her nose and her manic depression. Then I stood there praying with my eyes open, looking right at her, as I told her over and over that Jesus loved her.

She received it for a time, and then seemed to get a bit uncomfortable. I backed off, but should have just pressed through. The point of breakthrough is one moment past the place of being uncomfortable in Love. When people get uncomfortable, it isn't always bad. Love causes the shame, guilt, and unworthiness that we have hidden down in our hearts to squirm. When Love will not relent, these spirits cry out for from the depths for Him to stop. Love is just too good to receive sometimes.

Her eyes were wet, and I could see that God had touched her heart. Suddenly her hand went plunging into her pocket. She pulled out a wad of cash, and started trying to push it upon me in a desperate attempt to thank me. I told her that I wouldn't take it and that God's love was free. She persisted, but I didn't budge.

As I was backing up and telling her why I couldn't take the money, I noticed that the truck she came in was parked just a few feet away. The truck had a very old man in it. In her grocery bag she had all kinds of items used for sex, and I realized she intended to use them with this older man. The cash, the bag, the older man, and her physical beauty all made

me suddenly aware of the fact that she was selling her body to this man so that she could support her meth addiction.

As I walked toward my car and away from her, what I had just witnessed started to sink in, and my heart broke in two. God's emotions for His daughter started to overwhelm me, and tears started to fill my eyes. I was torn. On the one hand, God had revealed His love to this woman. Praise God. On the other hand, I didn't want her to get into that car and lose herself again. I wanted to put her in my car and drop her off at my mother's house so that someone could hug her until all the pain, devils, and brokenness left her.

Thank God He loves His kids more than we do. Sometimes this knowledge is all that consoles me when I witness the desperation in this world. He is in pursuit of every soul, especially the most broken. He desires that none should perish.

A lot of people shop at Walmart, but out of all the people there I was led to the woman who was selling her body to support her habit. That is no coincidence. If we are in God we will always find ourselves ministering to the most hurting, the most sick, the most lost, the most addicted, the most poor, and those who are most in need of Love.

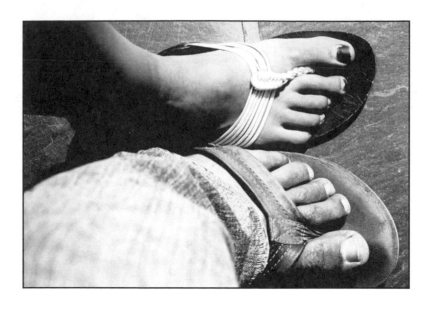

Simple Words

A few friends and I went to Walmart one day in hopes of finding people that we could love through the power of the Spirit. As we were walking in, the Lord gave me a picture of a woman with a gray sweatshirt, and I saw blue letters on the front. I asked Him what was wrong with her body, but I didn't get anything clearly. Instead of guessing what was wrong with her, I just decided to take what He had given me and make the most of it.

As I walked in, the first person I saw was a woman wearing a gray sweatshirt. The sweatshirt she was wearing didn't have blue letters on the front like I saw in the picture, but I took into consideration that while God speaks perfectly, I don't see or hear what He says perfectly. Paul said we see dimly and prophesy in part. I realized that she could be the woman He wanted me to pray for even though she didn't have blue letters on the front of her sweatshirt, so I went up to her and introduced myself.

After I briefly talked with her, I said that I felt that God wanted to heal her, and asked if there was something wrong with her body. She told me that she had tendon problems in her feet and that she had tried everything to make the pain go away, but nothing was working. She asked me why I wanted to know, and I told her about seeing a picture of her as I was praying. I asked her if I could pray for her feet, and she said, "Yes! I am willing to try anything at this point!"

I got down on my knees in the entryway of the store and started to release healing into her body. As I did, a woman who works at the store came over and laid hands on me in agreement of prayer. I was stoked. Things will happen if we step out! When we step out, others start to feel free and bold. We can blaze a trail for others to walk in.

As I finished praying I noticed that the woman I had been praying for, Tracy, had started to tear up. She thanked me in a heartfelt way, and I told her that if God gave me a picture of her and told me to find her, He must love her a lot. She received it, and I walked off. Sometimes I forget to have people try out the body part that was hurting to see if it was instantly healed. This time, like many times, I forgot.

I have learned that walking in faith is more important than having accuracy in a gift. Tracy wasn't wearing a sweatshirt that had blue letters on it like I saw, but nonetheless she was the one I was supposed to pray for.

The attaching of faith to the word is what makes it accurate, even if the word isn't very impressive. Learning to walk in boldness and faith is what pays off, not being super gifted by being able to tell someone his name or age or address. Any of us can do impressive things for God if we are willing to attach faith and boldness to what we hear.

Fruit That Will Last

I was waiting on God in the Walmart parking lot. I saw a quick flash of what I thought was a pineapple. I put that on the shelf. Then I saw a person with something wrapped around his or her head, like a bandana or something. I got up and went inside. I saw a woman in the produce department with a bandana wrapped around her head, though not exactly in the way that I had seen it in the picture.

I thought to myself, *Oh my gosh, if she is walking next to the pineapples, I am going to flip.* I got a better angle, and right as I did, she passed the pineapples. That was good enough for me. I went over to her and asked her if she had migraines, simply because the bandana in the picture was around her head. It was a shot in the dark. She said yes, and I prayed for her. She thanked me and left.

A word of knowledge doesn't need to be super specific. Just take what you have seen and draw some simple and to-the-point conclusions…like pineapples and migraines.

Also, be careful of the temptation while moving in the word of knowledge to write off words that seem less impressive than others. Pulling someone out of a wheelchair is more impressive than someone being healed of migraines, but we do not primarily do evangelism to see impressive miracles. Instead, we do evangelism so that God's love is revealed to people. When my motive is love, I find that I am just as excited about someone being healed of a headache as I am about the person who is healed of cancer.

A miracle is a sign. Signs, like the ones we use while driving our cars, point to something else and try to make us aware of a greater reality than the signs themselves. Miracles are a sign: They point to God. It is ridiculous to stand in awe of a sign when you can look at what the sign is pointing to. I don't get caught up on the size of the sign but on the beauty of the One the sign points to. If my motive is primarily love, any miracle (regardless of size) that takes place is incredibly valuable because God's love is demonstrated.

Bumper stickers that say "God loves you" and little metal fish that are plastered to the back of our cars don't get the message across to the majority of the unsaved population in the world that God loves them. But if you can heal someone in Jesus' name or tell her information about her life that only God would know, you will have her full attention. The people that you pray over will feel important to God and known by Him. Sometimes they even fall in love with Him.

God Stays up Late

Late one night, I went to Walmart and saw a picture of a young mother with short black hair holding up a baby girl and smiling at her. It was 2:00 A.M. The chance that there would be a mom in Walmart with a baby at 2:00 A.M. in the morning was hardy plausible. Most new mothers take every chance to sleep that they can get.

Tired, I went inside, skeptical that I would find anyone with short black hair. Even so, a woman with black hair was walking down the aisles with a baby in the shopping cart. It was hard to believe. I went up to her and told her that God said she was a good mom, and that He enjoyed that she enjoyed her daughter. She said thank you, and I left somewhat abruptly. It was late, and I was ready for bed.

Though we may not always understand what Holy Spirit tells us, and though what He tells us may not seem plausible in the least bit, we must trust Him and do as He says. He will test you through giving you

off-the-wall, obscure words for others. Sometimes He does this just to see if you will obey Him, and will watch to see if you have more fear of man than desire for Him. As you unquestioningly obey Him, He will pour out more accurate, specific words—but more importantly, you will receive more of Him.

Ministry isn't really about ministry. In the end, it is all about relationship with Him, even ministry. He tests us not just to see if He can give us more, but to help reveal to us the areas of our heart that are still susceptible to fear. He will use ministry to reveal the places in your heart that He desires to revolutionize with His love. He will challenge you to do things that are totally uncomfortable and outside your box, then He will watch to see if you decide to leap off the cliff, or cower back. If you jump, you won't just succeed at what He challenged you with, but you will also come closer to God Himself because faith is the vehicle we travel by to come closer to God. Take the leap. You will land in open arms.

Intrusive Love

On our way to Hawaii for our honeymoon, my wife and I entered into worship while we flew over the Pacific Ocean. As I was lost in love with Jesus, I saw a picture of a girl wearing a baby-blue shirt sitting and looking very sad. The word *cancer* was hovering over her.

I wasn't seeking the Lord for a word of knowledge. In fact, the word of knowledge came almost intrusively upon my time with Jesus. The reality is that when the first commandment is truly fulfilled in our lives, we naturally fulfill the second commandment to love people. While the first commandment needs to become *first* in the Church, God will not let us stay in our closet, either. If the first commandment is never fulfilled, we have missed the purpose to life. If the second commandment isn't fulfilled, we have to question if we ever fulfilled the first commandment to

begin with. Intimacy with Jesus causes us to become one with the Lord, and His heart for the lost becomes our own.

In faith I got up and walked the plane looking for a girl with a blue shirt on. After a few minutes of looking I found two girls, one with a baby-blue shirt on. It always surprises me when I find what I have seen in prayer, regardless of how many times I have had it happen previously. Nobody can know that information but God. The fact that we can actually hear from the God of the universe is absolutely astounding. It is an honor and mystery that is unfathomable.

I asked the girl with the blue shirt on if she or anyone else she knew had cancer. She didn't respond, so I asked her if cancer had caused her a great deal of sadness in her life. She quickly said no. I was disappointed, but glad that I tried.

Faith is spelled R-I-S-K. Hebrews says that it is impossible to please God without faith. I was in faith because I had just stepped out in risk, so I knew that I had pleased God, despite the picture seeming to be incorrect. God just wants us to try. If we try because of faith, He is pleased regardless of the outcome.

Later, as we were getting off the plane, the same girl asked me why I had asked her the questions that I did. I could have backed out and not told her the truth, but I decided to risk it again, possibly making me *and* God look stupid.

I told her, "I asked you that question because we were in prayer and I saw a picture of you. You looked sad, and the word *cancer* was written over you." She thanked me with an odd face, and my wife and I left. Despite two casts and no fish, I decided to keep my line in the water. I decided to continue to believe God that this picture was real and not worry about my two failed attempts. It is really easy to start to beat yourself up when you are moving in faith. It is easy to start to doubt yourself

and your ability to hear from God. I decided to stay in faith and not write off what I saw through disbelief, disqualification, or a lack of confidence in God's ability to speak to me. At the same time, I was content with nothing more happening.

My wife and I made our way to the baggage claim. As we were waiting for our bags, the same two girls approached me, making this our third interaction.

She asked me abruptly, "How did you know that about me?" She continued to tell me that her mom had died of cancer and that her best friend's mom was dying of cancer. At the mention of this, sadness swept over both of the girls' faces. She ended her explanation with the same question that she started with, "How did you know that about me?"

I told her that she is a daughter of God, and that the Lord revealed to me her situation because He wanted to touch her with His love and take her sadness away. I told her that He weeps with those who weep, and that He cared about her pain immensely. I asked them if my wife and I could pray with them. They said they would like that, so we grabbed their hands and prayed with them. I blessed her hurting heart and prayed healing for it and healing for her friend's mother.

His eye is on the sparrow. Surely then it is on His hurting child.

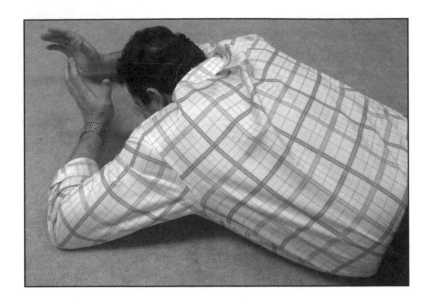

Shadow Healings

A few friends and I went to a local grocery store to do evangelism through words of knowledge. Without any words from God yet, we walked in and found a woman with a neck brace. To a Spirit-filled believer, something as blatant as wearing a neck brace in public is like painting a target on your shirt with "Come show me a miracle" written in the center of it.

We approached her and asked what happened to her neck. We talked with her for a while about her neck and the many other ailments she had. It turned out that her spinal problems were causing her body to be numb from the waist down.

She was a Christian and said she believed that God heals. The odd thing is that every time we would try to pray for her, she would skirt the issue and avoid it. If we did manage to start praying over her, she would

cut us off during prayer, change the subject, and say things like, "Amen to that brother," or "Thank you Jesus" so loud that the prayer we were praying was drowned out.

After a few instance like this, I realized that she was having a hard time receiving because of the religious lies that she had been fed. She didn't really believe what she said she believed or what she thought she believed. In her head she believed that God is good and that God wants to heal, but her heart had been kept from believing these truths by lies preached from podiums and bad past experiences.

I prayed for her anyway, and as we were praying together, another woman who had back and hip problems came over and asked us for prayer, too. Our group and the two women joined hands like a family would at dinner. I prayed a simple prayer of healing over both of them. As I did, it was as if I could sense Heaven open above us. The women didn't say anything. I don't think they felt a thing. I asked the woman with the back and hip problems how she felt. She started to bend over, touching her toes. I asked her if she could touch her toes before we prayed. She said, "I haven't been able to do that for 15 years! The pain was overwhelming before!" She was ecstatic.

As she was explaining how amazed she was over what had just happened, a man walked up to our little Holy Ghost huddle. He leaned over to me and asked, "What are you guys doing?" I replied, "We were praying." He said, "That is amazing."

I didn't know what he meant by that. What was amazing? Who was he? Why was he talking to us?

He said, "I was on the other side of the store a few minutes ago. As I was shopping I walked by you guys and suddenly the back problems that I have had for 20 years vanished. I am healed!"

God healed a man simply by him walking past us. That struck me with awe. The Holy Spirit is so much more powerful, expansive, and thorough than we know! This man's healing showed me that we can allow the Presence of God to fill us to such a degree that we can simply walk past sick people and they will be healed. That is remarkable. Think of walking through hospitals focused on God, and as you pass their doorways, patient after patient comes out into the hallways wondering, "What invisible Doctor just restored me?"

Peter's shadow and Paul's touch did the same kind of thing (see Acts 5:15; 28:8). This means that people don't need to understand healing, prayer, faith, or even God's goodness in order for them to be healed. Yes, those things help, but as long as unbelief is not present, God will heal them. Faith does not need to be present in a person to effect a miracle, as long as unbelief is not present. The Holy Spirit can be strong enough in us to effect a miracle before people ever even have the faith for it.

The Holy Spirit lives in you. You carry the Presence of the Holy Spirit to an incredible degree. He who is in you is greater than that which is outside you. God is very big in you. Demons shudder when you enter the room. When you are driving on the freeway and you pass a person in their car who has cancer, it starts to die. If you will believe that God is strong in you, He will begin to reveal Himself as such. Shadow healings like the one that happened in the store will happen in your life if you believe for them. Likewise, if you believe that the Holy Spirit isn't really that impressive in you and only convicts people of sin, comforts people, and helps people read the Bible, then that is all you will find Him to be. If you believe, you will receive.

I told the man what had just happened to the woman with the back and hip problems. It turned out that she was his wife. He went on to tell me that they had just moved into the area. The night before he had been down on his knees in desperate prayer, telling the Lord that the pain

in his back was becoming more than he could handle. He told the Lord that he couldn't go on unless He healed him. He then asked the Lord where his family should attend church. The Lord told him that the next day he would meet a young man in the store, and that this young man would tell him where to attend church.

My wife and I were attending Bethel Church at the time, and I happened to have one of their cards in my back pocket, so I pulled it out and gave it to him. We both stood there for a second in disbelief as to what had just happened.

The woman with the neck brace was still standing there. She now had feeling in her feet that she hadn't had for years, but she wasn't very impressed with that. Her unbelief and bad doctrine were blocking her ability to receive what Jesus died for.

To faith-filled believers, a partial healing means God is doing something; so jump on the bandwagon full force and pray a second time.

To religious Christians, a partial healing is confusing and convinces them that it wasn't really God's will to heal in that particular situation. Their prayer of faith comes to a halt and they give up. Like the unstable man described in the first chapter of James, they surrender in prayer, then usually experience a feeling of failure and disappointment. This disappointment mars their desire to pray for healing the next time they encounter disease. Even Jesus experienced a partial healing when He prayed for a blind man in Mark 8:22-26. Jesus prayed once more and the man was completely restored. Jesus didn't stop praying when the miracle didn't happen the first time. He knew God's will had not changed despite the circumstances.

It felt like the woman with the neck brace was holding on to her diseases. It is sad how bad teaching about God distorts our thinking and keeps us from the very thing that God desires to give us. I don't like

leaving a person unimpressed with God, believer or not, so more needed to happen before I felt a peace about leaving this woman.

Thankfully, a woman on our team named Chelsea wisely took the woman aside and ignored the plethora of physical problems that the woman had. Instead, she spoke out prophetic words to the woman's heart rather than about her body. In a few moments, the woman was in tears at the revelation of God's love. Her family life was falling apart, and she needed to know that God was still in the midst of it.

Chelsea saw that the way to get a fresh revelation of God's love into this woman's heart was not through getting her healed physically. Through God supernaturally revealing things about her life that only He knew, the woman's fading belief that God was still in the midst of her family's problems was affirmed.

The goal is love, not a miracle. But love is best demonstrated supernaturally rather than talked about. This means that love is most loving when it comes through supernatural means and is filled with power. Anything less is less than what the men and women in the Bible settled for.

Bell-Bottoms and Harleys

Adam and I were on a treasure hunt. We knew God wanted to pull gold out of some people, so we went looking for them. We prayed and worshiped, and God told us to go to a local pet store. I saw a picture of a woman, who seemed to have back pain, wearing pants that looked somewhat like bell-bottoms. I thought to myself, *Thirty-five years late, God.*

Adam confirmed the word of knowledge about back pain. He had sensed the same thing as we prayed.

We went in right as the pet store was closing, and the only two people in the store were a huge Harley Davidson rider and his girl. Believe it or not, she had pants that flared out at the bottom. They were walking out the door, so we chased them down and asked the woman if she had back pain. She did. We prayed for them and blessed them.

Blessing others is an extremely important facet of the Christian life that most believers do not understand. We have the authority to bless or to curse with our words. Our words carry power on them, so much so that Proverbs 18:21 tells us, "Death and life are in the power of the tongue...." This is a literal statement. We either speak life over people by blessing them or we destroy them with the power that God has given us in our words.

The apostle Peter was given extraordinary power that was meant to build up the newly born Church in Acts. The covenant of grace was a new idea to Peter, and he reverted back to a mindset of law and death when he misused his authority with Ananias and Sapphira in Acts 5:1-11. Like any good leader would do, Peter could have taken Ananias and Sapphira aside and calmly talked to them about their error in keeping some of their money from the apostles when they sold some property. In doing so, Peter's kindness would have led them to repentance and the situation would have been redeemed. Instead, he functioned out of law and punishment and spoke out words of judgment on this couple. In doing so, Peter mistakenly called down judgment upon them. Curses can occur any time our declarations, words, and thoughts do not line up with the heart of God about another person. Our words and judgments about others can physically affect them (as well as emotionally and spiritually), even to the point of death.

Most of the Church reads the story of Ananias and Sapphira differently than what is presented above, but if you think that God killed Ananias and Sapphira like the majority of the Church does, you are mistaken. Jesus took all the punishment and wrath of God upon Himself when He died on the cross. If you truly believe that like you profess you do, then you will read the New Testament in light of that belief. You will stop blaming God for killing people who are less than perfect—people like you and me. Again, Jesus already bore the punishment for our sins when He died on the cross. We are unpunishable.

I used to read Acts 5 in a way that tried to justify God killing Ananias and Sapphira by the severity of their sin. Then I realized that God forgives rapists, child molesters, murderers, and abusive spouses today, so surely He forgives people for not giving all the money that they appear to be giving. If He killed Ananias and Sapphira for a sin as small as keeping some of their own money for themselves, then you and I should be toast.

For years I thought that the fear that swept over the Church after Ananias and Sapphira died was a pure and holy thing. I realize now that I was wrong. Having fear that God will kill you if you sin is not only an incorrect belief about God, but it will also never bring you closer in relationship with God. The fear of God and the fear that God will kill you if you sin could not be further in likeness from one another. The former comes from Heaven, the latter from hell.

I no longer read Scripture in a way that does not affirm in my heart the overwhelming reality of God's goodness. In doing so, I changed the way I read Acts 5 and was struck with the reality of the power of our words.

We must never lack in choosing to bless others, even if we don't agree with them. Anything else is not the will and heart of God. Since we are called to bless our enemies, surely we are to bless those that we merely do not agree with. Blessing others isn't condoning what they are doing; it is using the authority and power God has given us to invite Him to do what is best for them. Blessing others is also a form of resisting control. It forces us to take our hands off a situation and give it to God. We can either choose to bless or to curse. There isn't a middle ground. In withholding blessings because of disagreement, you naturally leave a void that should be filled with a blessing. Choose to bless and relinquish control, or find yourself cursing.

Even tough Harley riders light up like a bulb when real blessings are involved. After we prayed for his woman and he saw that we were

genuine in our care, he became soft and joyful. They thanked us for pray-ing for them, and walked away feeling good about life and about Jesus.

The unsaved world doesn't need judgment and criticism; they need kindness that will lead them to repentance. After all, was it God's anger and wrath that brought you to your knees in repentance of sin, or was it the fact that He showed His love to you by sending His son to die for you, despite your problems?

From Iraq to Awe

O nce I was in a store while doing some outreach with the youth. A young man walked past me and I heard the Lord say, "Talk to him. He is very discontented with his life." I had a sheet of words of knowledge but he didn't seem to be on the sheet.

I started talking to him, and he asked me what we were doing in the store. I told him that we get pictures and visions of people and what is wrong with their bodies, write them down on a sheet of paper, and then go into the store to find the people. Once we find each person we release healing on him or her

He said, "Really? That is pretty weird. Why do you do this?" I said, "Just to love people." "Are you gay?" he asked. I laughed and pointed to my wife walking by. He said, "OK, you aren't gay, and you do this for free. What is the catch?" I told him, "Nothing. We enjoy doing it."

He looked at me with an odd face as his eyes looked down and focused on the paper that I was holding in my hands. With one swift swipe, he snagged the paper out of my hands and started to read over what I had written down. I felt somewhat exposed. Humiliation set in because I knew that he wasn't on my sheet, yet I was talking to him, which I thought would look phony from his perspective.

He pointed to one of the descriptions that I had on the sheet and said, "Oh, there I am. Wow, that is crazy that you knew about my shoulder and even the specific shirt that I am wearing!"

He was on my sheet, though I hadn't realized it until he pointed it out. I was relieved. He began to share that he had just recently come back from the Middle East, fighting in the Army. He had seen a lot of his friends die, and as a result didn't believe God existed. He reasoned that if God did exist, he didn't want to know Him anyway because He had let his friends die. If he had ever believed God was good, he didn't anymore.

I asked him, "If God heals you today, would you not only believe God exists, but that He is good?" He said, "Yeah, I guess I would have to."

I asked him if I could lay my hand on him as I prayed. He told me that would make him uncomfortable. I said, "No problem. The Holy Ghost will heal you just standing near us." I started praying for him with my eyes open, looking right at him. I pointed at his shoulder and commanded it to be healed.

When I finished praying, I said, "Try it out. Try to do something with your shoulder that you couldn't do before." He stood there, motionless. Thinking he hadn't heard me, I said it again. He said, "No." I asked him why he wouldn't try out his shoulder. He said, "Because what if I am healed?" I said, "Then you have some changing to do, don't you?" He smiled, and tried moving his shoulder and arm.

His shoulder must have been better, because he began cussing a lot after he started moving it. Not only did his shoulder impress him, but he was also struck that someone cared enough to pray for him in a public place. Bad words spilled from his mouth, not used negatively toward me or the Lord, but in astonishment. The curse words had a purity to them despite their vulgarity because it was the only way he knew to express awe and wonder at what God had done. I asked him what he couldn't do before we prayed. Referring to his recent movements, he said, "That."

I started prophesying to him about his heart and his life and prayed for him again. I was about to leave when he stopped me and said, "Seriously man? You just pull me aside, a total stranger, tell me about my life and what is wrong with my body, pray for me, and I get healed. Then you tell me that God is good and in doing so totally freak me out, and for what? Why?"

I smiled at him and replied, "Because God loves you."

Cancer, Bow

A man who was in the military came into the Healing Rooms. He was candid, unemotional, and even a bit unfriendly. But I love the army guys. They are that way because they are just scared. They have been trained in law, not grace. They are the type of guys who cry like babies at the drop of a hat after experiencing God's love.

As he walked into the room I distinctly felt pain in my throat. I realized that I was experiencing a word of knowledge, though not like I normally received them. This word of knowledge I felt *physically* rather than *seeing* it. We didn't start out the casual, calm way that we normally do when we are praying for the sick. I just asked him point blank what was wrong with his throat. Eyebrow raised, he said that he had been diagnosed with cancerous cysts in his throat only a week before. We prayed for him and he left.

The next week, in came the same guy, but this time he was excited to see me, happy, even childishly playful. He was bouncing as he walked up to me and lightly slapped me on the back like a friend he had known for a dozen years.

He told me that the doctor had done a scan a few days after we prayed and couldn't find any cancer. When the doctor asked what he had done to get rid of the cancer, which had been there only days before, he boldly said, "Jesus" in his typical military tone.

God speaks in many different ways. Like anything else in life, we are rarely endowed skills that are not learned. We learn to play the piano, communicate, and ride a bike through trying to do it over and over. After time, we get better at it. Likewise, to become more accurate at hearing God's voice, it helps to learn how He primarily speaks to *you*. Is it through visions, pictures, hearing, smell, feelings, or dreams? You will find that God is not limited in the ways He communicates with His people. He can use the Bible or choose not to use it. He can speak through an unsaved, unredeemed person. He can speak through animals (Numbers 22:28), trances (Acts 10:10), weather (Jonah 1:4-12), fire (1 Kings 18:38) and gentle whispers (1 Kings 19:12). Learn how you hear from Him most often, and listen intently. He will tell you secrets never revealed to any other person in all of history.

Miracles

*Does God give you His Spirit and work
miracles among you because you observe the law,
or because you believe what you heard?*
(Galatians 3:5)

*For I will not presume to speak of anything except what Christ
has accomplished through me, resulting in the obedience of the
Gentiles by word and deed, in the power of signs and wonders, in
the power of the Spirit; so that from Jerusalem and round about
as far as Illyricum I have fully preached the gospel of Christ.*
(Romans 15:18-19 NASB)

Discard All Aid to Hear

We were in the Healing Rooms praying for people. An elderly man came in with his wife, who told us that he needed healing for his ears. We didn't know how bad his hearing was until he took out his hearing aids. This guy was stone deaf. We had to yell at him to communicate once he took out his aids.

One of my spiritual fathers, Marc Buchheit, grabbed the anointing oil and soaked the ends of his index fingers with it. Before I knew it, Marc had stuck his fingers in this man's ears, oil and all. As Marc prayed for this man's healing, I observed the wife on the other side of the room. She had dealt with this deafness for over a dozen years, having to yell frequently just to communicate with the love of her life. The frustration that she had experienced on a daily basis must have been trying, to say the least.

After Marc had bound a deaf spirit on this man, we asked him if his hearing had improved. It hadn't. When he yelled, "What did you say?" it was clear just how much effect our prayer had made. No worries, God hadn't changed His mind about buying this man's healing by sending Jesus to the cross to die. God's will was still to heal him.

Marc had me pray this time. I prayed with all the fervency that I had. Nothing happened. Marc prayed again. Nothing.

At this point I got uncomfortable. This guy was *not* getting healed, but Marc seemed completely undeterred by the circumstances. In fact, Marc became more provoked to pray each time the guy didn't get healed. The violent take it by force.

Marc prayed a fourth time. Then he had the man stand a few feet away, facing us. Marc yelled out, "OK, repeat back to me what I say." Marc loosely covered his mouth with his hand so that the man couldn't read his lips and in a normal voice said, "God is good."

It still blows my mind when I remember this moment. The man's eyes widened suddenly and he blurted out, "You said God is good!"

Marc, unaffected by the man's surprise, told the man to take five steps backward. Now they were about 20 feet apart. He covered his mouth again, but this time said, "Jesus loves you." Again, the man excitedly repeated exactly what Marc had said. The wife started to squirm with hope on the other side of the room. Clearly they were making headway.

Marc still didn't seem impressed. He wanted more for the man. He told the man to walk to the corner of the room that was diagonal from where he was standing. They were standing 20 feet apart now. Then he told the man to face the corner. Marc covered his mouth again, despite the fact that the man wasn't even facing us and couldn't see us. Later Marc told me that he does this so that scoffers and people without faith can't say the man used a reflection off the posters on the walls to read his lips.

This time Marc didn't use a normal voice. He whispered, "Jesus healed me." The man spun around and yelled, "You said Jesus healed me! HE DID!"

In that instant, the man's wife fell to the ground weeping in thankfulness. I stood there in shock as I tried to grasp what had just happened. I looked over and saw Lydia, Marc's wife, on the floor holding the wife of the man. Marc was already moving on to pray for the next person. He is used to fantastic miracles.

If you have never seen Jesus open the ears of the deaf, I am so sorry. It was one of the most amazing things I have ever seen, and I wish that every person could have seen it.

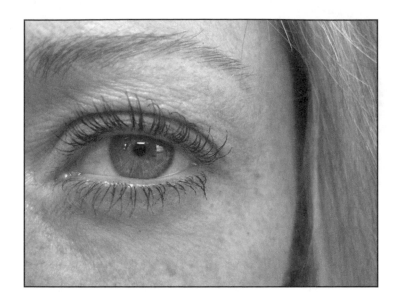

Once Lost, Now Found

I was ministering at a small conference on healing and prophetic evangelism in Wenatchee, Washington, along with a few others. The crowd was asking us questions about the healing ministry, and we were giving answers to them over the microphone.

After 30 minutes of us sharing Scripture and telling stories of times God had moved miraculously on our behalf, a young woman stood up on the front row. She shared that she had recently given her life to Jesus and that our stories had opened her heart to believe that God could heal her.

I asked her what needed healing. She shared that she had been completely blind in her left eye since birth.

After we were done speaking and answering questions, a group of us surrounded this young woman to pray for her. We broke a spirit of blindness off of her, then had her cover her good eye with her hand so that

she could not see out of it. A man waved his arm in front of her face and said, "What do you see?"

As tears started streaming down her face, she told us that she could see an arm waving in front of her face. I looked at her left eye and noticed that it would follow my hand as I moved it in front of her face, when prior to prayer it did not.

Some of the people standing around started to get excited, even shouting. Understandably so. They had just witnessed a miracle right before their eyes. My heart was beating quickly as well.

Just to affirm what had just happened, I said, "Wait a second. Let me get this straight. You could NOT see out of this eye ever? You weren't just colorblind? You were totally blind?" This precious soul looked at me with mascara smeared all over her face and said, "Yes. I was totally blind, and now I can see."

The hymn "Amazing Grace" rang out in my head as I asked her another question, "What do you see now?" She communicated that though she could see, she couldn't see clearly yet. I was reminded of the time when Jesus prayed for the blind man who saw something like trees walking about after the first prayer. Jesus prayed again and the man's vision was completely restored so that it wasn't blurry anymore.

So we prayed again. This time, we held up a hand in front of her face and asked her to tell us how many fingers she saw. We held up three, and she said three. Four, and she said four. When we help up one and she said "One," the room exploded. Exuberant, uninhibited, involuntary praise started to rise from the room in shouts, laughter, and quiet prayers.

I asked her to read the banner on the back wall. She read it for all to hear, "Jesus died for me."

As people were hugging her and looking at her restored eye, I walked to the other side of the room where people were standing who had

never witnessed a miracle take place right before their eyes. They had come unsure of what to expect from our time together, and now stood motionless with their jaws on the floor. One woman pulled me aside and said, "I have never seen anything like this. I believe God does miracles, but I had never *seen* a miracle…until today." I said, "This is who God is," as I pointed toward the young woman who had just received a new eye.

Miracles reveal God's character. A miracle is a statement from Heaven, a declaration as to *who* God is. He loves to heal His children. He is good.

God of Creation, Present

My wife and I were in Tijuana, Mexico, on a short-term mission trip with Bethel Church. Toward the end of the trip, Christine and I spent the day on Revolution Street. Around noon we sat down at a restaurant to have lunch.

An older woman came up to our table to beg. She was dirty and her hair was matted. Her skin had been burned by the hot sun more than once and had turned its color to a deep brown with a reddish hue. The deep creases on her cheeks and around her eyes and mouth showed her age. She was beautiful.

The waiter told her that she had to leave and needed to let us eat. It reminded me of the times my dad shamed our dog to stop him from coming to the dinner table to beg for scraps of food as our family ate. That is appropriate for a dog but never for a human being.

So, we invited her to eat with us. We fed her, held her hand, and spoke to her the kindest words that we could with our limited vocabulary. When we got stuck in telling her how beautiful and valuable she was, we called over the waiter who had told her to leave and asked him to interpret for us. We made sure that the same mouth that shamed her was now used to honor and love her.

She told us that she was sick, so we prayed for her. She told us that as we prayed an intense heat swept through her body. After the heat left, she told us that she felt strength again. The sickness was gone.

From the moment we invited her to sit with us, everyone else began to treat her with love, instead of as a piece of trash. It is remarkable how much influence each one of us has. We must use it to get others to respect and love those whom they won't otherwise. We bought her a rose, gave her some money, and blessed her. She ate all her food. By the end of our time she came around the table and started crying as she held us. She kissed us over and over and said, "You are the people of God" while tears wetted the dry, cracked skin on her face. She kept lightly patting Christine's pregnant tummy while holding us. We were so blessed.

As we were eating, a man who was drunk saw us interacting with this wonderful woman and came over. We talked with him, discovered he was an atheist, and offered to pray with him. Our prayer consisted only of us blessing him.

When he was leaving he said, "I don't believe in God, but would you keep praying for me?" I laughed really hard. It seemed to be a fundamentally contradictive statement that he had just made. Instead of trying to debate him into the Kingdom I said, "You may not believe in God, but you believe in Love, don't you?" He said, "Yes, of course." I told him, "Then you believe in God." He smiled and said, "Pray for me. Please keep praying for me."

When night came, Christine and I made our way to a stage that was set up for people to perform in the middle of Revolution Street. Our group had rented the stage for the sole purpose of preaching the Gospel. Our team went up on stage right after a group of transvestites had finished performing. What a perfect place to preach the Gospel! And our team did. It was fiery. I loved it. Hagglers walked by and yelled, and demoniacs stormed the crowd and tried to cause distractions.

I watched one man in particular. He wouldn't come up and get prayer, though people were getting healed up front. I couldn't tell if he was desperate or critical. I started talking to him. His name was Christopher and he was desperate. As he shared his story with me, I could feel God filling me with compassion for him. He had just lost his uncle, his only remaining family member, who had faithfully loved him for years until the day he died. Then his wife of 15 years was deported suddenly to Argentina and wouldn't be back to visit for three years. He also had schizophrenia and was addicted to crystal meth, cigarettes, and coffee. He was in a downward spiral and didn't know what to do, but was desperate.

I calmly asked him if he believed what the people were proclaiming from the stage. He said he was OK with it, but didn't know why God let all this stuff happen to him. It was the age-old fight: "Is God good?" Christopher, like the majority of people on earth, needed to be convinced of God's goodness again. He was convinced God wasn't good because of the circumstances in his life. Fortunately, God likes convincing people otherwise.

I asked him if he wanted to be rid of his bitterness toward the Lord and if he would be willing to ask God for help to get out of his mess. He said he didn't want to be bitter anymore and he wanted help, but he didn't know if God could help him. I asked him if he wanted to give God a chance to help him. I literally asked him, "What if you just give Jesus a try?"

Earlier in my life I would have shuddered at such a non-committal form of evangelism. I don't worry about it anymore. I know that when I get a chance to pray, God will show up and touch the person. Once touched, the person commits their life to Jesus out of desire rather than out of the sobriety of counting the cost in committing to a religion.

He said yes. He was willing to give Jesus a try. Using the open door Christopher had just given me, I had him verbally surrender his bitterness toward God through prayer, then confess with his mouth that God loved him and had only the best for him. I had him ask Jesus into his heart and ask God to forgive him of his sins. He got born again.

Then we both started to cry. We were just holding each other as I prayed over him, both of us weeping. It was supernatural compassion. Compassion—real, broken compassion—is powerful. The trust it builds between two people is amazing, and the action it causes a person to take is remarkable. True compassion is different from sympathy or pity, counterfeits of compassion. True compassion always leads the person into change. To Christ, compassion was a gateway to power. When compassion came upon Jesus, it always resulted in healing the sick or raising the dead. Real love is movement. Compassion without action is simply heartwarming emotions, and it doesn't help people.

We ended our time of prayer and wiped the tears from our eyes. I looked into his face and saw that though he was saved, he was still hurting, broken, and in bondage. I didn't know what else to do to help him, so I shook his hand and left. As I walked away, I felt my stomach churn as I realized that Christopher hadn't seen God's goodness demonstrated to him in a tangible way yet. He still had all of his problems, and his circumstances were still exactly the same as before we prayed. I hadn't helped him tangibly in the least bit! Though he had received Jesus, he hadn't seen or felt Jesus. What God wanted to do that night in his life wasn't accomplished yet, and I was walking away! Sure, Christopher had a ticket to

Heaven, but how long would he hold on to it without his faith resting on the power of God rather than my words? Paul talked about the imperativeness of this in First Corinthians 2:4-5. Would his ticket slip out of his hand as he reached up to steady his head from the schizophrenia, or as he wept over his lost wife, or his uncle, or as he reached for the drugs that he hated? He needed something that changed his life in a practical way, not just tears.

I went back to find him, and he was gone. I started crying more, unnerved by what I had just done, or better said, the lack of what I had done. I was weeping. After some time I looked back to the spot where I had met him, and he was standing there again. I went over to him and asked if Christine and my friend Reese could pray over him and soak him in prayer. He said that if I trusted them, he trusted them.

A few minutes into prayer, another Bethel student joined them to pray for Christopher. Christopher mentioned that he didn't have good eyesight, so Reese began to command healing in Christopher's eyes. Nothing happened. We prayed again. One of the students started getting a little invasive, or so it felt to me. I wanted to rise up and protect Christopher, and had to hold back from pulling this Bethel student away from Christopher. All he seemed to care about was getting a healing, but something told me to let it go and trust the Lord in this guy.

What a tragedy it would have been if I had discouraged this young man. In actuality, it was disbelief in me that was making me want to pull him away from Christopher. If I had really believed that God would heal Christopher, it wouldn't matter what means it would take to get him healed. If I had been full of faith, I would have trusted the Lord and let this guy do anything to Christopher that he felt led to do. The real issue didn't have to do with me trusting the guy standing in front of Christopher. The real issue was my deficiency in trusting the Lord in the situation.

This is one reason pastors can become controlling when they are trying to protect their flock.

They prayed a third time for his eyes and again nothing happened. Suddenly Christopher said, "That is odd. I have had emphysema for years, and it is gone suddenly. My lungs are clear, and I can breathe very well. That never happens." He was very calm as he told us this. He showed us an inhaler that he took out of his pocket, telling us that he hadn't informed us about his other physical problems just to see what God would do through us without us knowing about his problems. We had prayed for his eyes and his lungs got healed. Go figure.

We prayed for his eyes a fourth time. This time he said, "Well, God must have a sense of humor. My eyes are a little better, but more importantly, my knee is better!" He lifted his pant leg to show us a 7-inch scar down his knee. He told us that his kneecap had been blown off by a piece of shrapnel in Vietnam. He now had a fake kneecap, and everyday for the last 25 years it had caused him pain. He had to take Vicodin multiple times a day for it, and was addicted to it as a result. Now, the pain was completely gone for the first time in 25 years. He started bending his knee and trying it out. He bent it all the way, with all of his weight on it. No pain. To be honest, I was shocked.

I asked him how he would know if God gave him a new kneecap since the one that he had was fake. He told me that fake kneecaps don't pop, so if his knee popped, he would know it was new. So we prayed for a new kneecap. I reached up into Heaven and just acted like I was grabbing a new kneecap from Heaven, then put that same hand on his knee. When we finished praying, he started squatting, trying out his knee. Amazingly, his knee popped! It hadn't popped in 25 years. God gave him a new kneecap. Why not? If He created the whole earth, He can create a new bone.

Christopher had told us before we started praying that he was naturally a very calm, unexpressive person. He didn't want us to be disheartened when we prayed for him and he didn't get fanatical. But after we prayed he was clearly excited. He also became convinced that what I had told him about God was true. Now he knew that God really could take care of his other problems as well. He told us, "You have made a believer out of me" and "My wife is never going to believe me." We were ecstatic. We blessed him, gave him a Bible, and he told us that he wanted to go read it right then.

Moments before he left to go read the Word, he got really scared for his wife, realizing that she wasn't saved and that without Jesus she would go to hell. We didn't say a thing about hell to him. He just realized that it was true without anyone scaring him into it. He said, "I have to tell her! Oh God, let her live until I have the chance to tell her! God, don't let anything happen to her!" We assured him that everything would be OK, and we prayed for her to be brought back to him.

The reality is that Christopher wouldn't have been convinced of God's goodness without us praying for his healing in faith. He would have been saved, but wouldn't have known that God loved him in his heart. He would have believed it because you are supposed to. He would have believed it because that is what other people told him. However, the moment he was healed, God's love wasn't a far off, immaterial idea. God's love became tangible to him the moment he was healed.

We must make God's love tangible to those around us. We must demonstrate God's love rather than just talk about it. When we just talk about God's love and don't demonstrate it, we leave people in a place of trusting our words rather than trusting God themselves.

Christopher believed that God was good because I told him so. He and I had built trust between us, so he believed what I said. That is the only reason why he believed. His belief in God was rooted in me. But the

moment God healed him, his relationship and faith in God became his own. I was no longer needed to tell him that God was good, because God showed Christopher Himself.

We must demonstrate the Kingdom. Without it, people's faith is frail and easily destroyed. What is faith? That God is good. We must *show* them that He is good.

Salvations

The High School

I am a substitute teacher at our local high school. When I started teaching, I determined in my heart that I would not succumb to fear and would overtly share Jesus in my secular classrooms. The fear of losing one's job can never be prioritized over fulfilling the Great Commission. I decided that I would be bold about my faith even if that meant I lost my job. Not religious, but bold. The difference is vast.

Religion is that which the Pharisees and Sadducees walked in. Religion is what caused them to think that they loved God and served Him, though they killed Him when He revealed Himself on earth. Religion is a contradiction that is justified by those who are in it.

I once saw a shirt that said, "Religion is an organized system or institution of belief based upon the traditions of man instead of the pursuit of friendship with God. Religion is the act of playing church,

exchanging internal truths for external performance, substituting spiritual realities with carnal rituals." God likes that shirt.

Yes, the Bible says that pure and undefiled religion is to care for the orphan and the widow, but the reason why James tells this to us is because, in and of itself, religion is incredibly fallen and detestable in God's eyes (see James 1:27). James is clarifying to us that religion is defiled and impure in nature, but it can be redeemed by caring for the poor in spirit. If a person learns to truly care for the poor in spirit, they have come into friendship with God, which means that religion is losing its grip on their life. Let us not justify living in the law because of one misinterpreted verse in the New Testament.

I have found that people hate religion, but they rarely have a problem with Jesus. If they have a problem with Jesus, it is only because we— or someone before us—were being religious in our presentation of Him. Nobody will turn away genuine Love. It is the built-in need of every human heart.

Christians crack me up. They try to share Jesus religiously with someone and when the person isn't interested or is even somewhat revolted, they shake the dust off their shoes and move on. They act like Lot and never look back, waiting for the judgment of God to fall. They reassert to themselves their belief in predestination, and are comforted with the thought that it wasn't their presentation that was the problem, but that the person they just talked to was predetermined to not accept God.

Unbelievers aren't the ones with the problem. We are. If we get out of religion and into friendship with God, we will find that the lost and broken are naturally drawn to us. Sinners loved Jesus and enjoyed being with Him. He didn't try to change them; He just loved them and demonstrated the Kingdom. In doing so, they were changed. Prostitutes, robbers, and the poor loved being with Jesus. It was the religious, the Christians of His day, who couldn't stand Jesus.

Because I had determined to share my faith overtly in the classroom, I had to figure out a nonreligious way to do so. I decided to start sharing miracle stories with my classes after they got their work done. I would tell them about times when God healed the sick through me, or worked some sort of fabulous miracle. Sometimes it was uncomfortably silent when I was done. Other times the whole class stood as they loudly cheered and applauded God. I often had students approach me in tears after I told a story, telling me that they needed prayer or wanted to rededicate their lives back to Jesus.

This went on for longer than a year. I was doing the very thing that I was assured by many would get me fired, but no complaints ever came from any of my students or their parents. I had witches, atheists, drug addicts, and kids who had been sexually abused in my classes. None of them had a problem with God's love.

After time, I had substituted in enough classes at the high school that every student enrolled had heard a miracle story. Shelton High is not a small school either. I was very pleased, and was thankful to God for backing me as I stepped out, but I started asking God to take it to another level. I wanted to see more students saved and healed in my classes. I started to ask God to give me words of knowledge for my students. One afternoon, He especially surprised me.

I was sitting at my desk as my students came into the classroom and started their daily silent sustained reading. The Holy Spirit clearly spoke to me, highlighting a young woman in the classroom, and said, "She is ready to receive Me. Ask her." I hadn't personally interacted with this young woman before and I had no knowledge about her life or where she was at in her journey with God.

I got up and went over to her desk. I took a leap of faith and simply asked, "Is it time for you to receive Jesus?" Her eyes widened and grew

wet in the same moment. She nodded. I told her to come to my desk when the period was over.

In the four-minute window of time between classes, Jazzy received Jesus as the Lord of her life and was born again. Leaving the classroom with a glow that she didn't possess when she entered, she headed to her next class. She even made it there on time.

I have learned that we simply don't ask enough. Many times all we have to do is ask and someone will be born again. How can asking hurt? I don't mean being intrusive, but just gently asking someone if they want to know Jesus. Many times we stay in relationship with people who don't know Jesus, hoping that our lifestyle will somehow convince them that they need to follow Jesus. After ten years of not simply asking them, we realize something is awry. If we don't overtly tell them about Jesus or show them a supernatural demonstration of the Gospel, such as healing them or releasing the Holy Spirit's peace on them, we aren't even giving them a fighting chance to figure out the Good News.

I can say that 95 percent of the time when I have simply asked people if they want more of God, if they want to feel God, or if they want to know Jesus, they say yes. We just need to ask. It isn't as hard as we think to lead someone to Heaven.

The Reindeer People

It was my second time in Mongolia. This time our team was headed to the Reindeer (Tsataan) people in the northernmost portion of the country. The Tsataan were a nomadic people who had received their name from their complete reliance on their reindeer for milk, meat, and transportation to move their teepees from their summer camp to their winter camp.

These people had not yet received the Gospel, and we had been told that no one had ever told them about the Good News in Jesus. A local missionary named Scott, who was coming with us to help translate and be our guide during our adventure, had been dreaming of going to the Tsataan people for years. He was extremely excited.

Traveling to these people by car was impossible because of the rough terrain of the path that led through the mountains to their teepees.

We drove our Russian vans as far as the road would permit us, then met up with a local man who owned 20 horses. We had already been traveling by van on the incredibly bumpy dirt roads for two days, and for the next three days we would be on horseback until we arrived at the Tsataan's home. Some people on the team weren't looking forward to this, but I was.

The ride was beautiful, even breathtaking. We would plot our course by pointing to the mountain farthest away on the horizon, then riding until we reached it. Once we stood in its shadow, our guide would pick the next mountain to aim for, and we would start riding again. We slept under the stars and drank from clear mountain streams. I felt like Frodo in *The Lord of the Rings*.

After days of riding, we looked up and spotted white teepees far off in the distance. We rode up to the people, greeted them, gave them gifts, and set up camp. We planned on spending three days with them.

After we had put our tents up and had eaten something, our leader gathered us together in one of the Tsataan teepees. As I looked at some of the people sitting around the tent I realized that as a whole they were dismal, depressed, and generally unhappy. With the chief of the tribe present, we told them our intentions in coming all that way to be with them. We talked about Jesus and exhorted them to follow Him and Him alone.

An anvil of steel couldn't have dropped to the ground more quickly than our words did. For whatever reason, these people thoroughly distrusted us, and our words had little effect on their hearts as a result. The chief even told us, "This belief system is for children. We will never follow Jesus." He repeated himself more than once in different ways as his people firmly stood with him. They couldn't have been clearer about where they stood. It was uncomfortable to say the least.

After that interaction the team became extremely discouraged. We began wondering why God had sent us on a five-day journey just to get to the people and have them totally reject the Gospel. I went to bed thinking about how a long-term missionary needed to come live with these people in order to build relationships with the people and develop some trust. Building trust would take months, maybe even years.

In those days I didn't understand faith. If something didn't work out, I would jump ship and make a new spiritual plan. Thinking that a long-term missionary needed to come is an example of how I dealt with problems. We had planned to be with the Tsataan for three days. We had felt that God wanted us to take this trip in order that they receive salvation—not later, but while we were there. In thinking that a long-term missionary needed to come live with these people in order for them to get saved, I was demonstrating my inability to stay in faith and stick to the plan that God had given us. Faith presses on until God's words come to pass despite the circumstances.

Fortunately, our leader knew that God had sent us to these people and held firmly to what he had heard from God. While the rest of us were tossed around like waves on the sea (see James 1:6-8), Jimmy was resolutely steady. He got up early the next morning and sought God on the mountaintop for a solution.

The team woke up disillusioned and defeated, myself included. Jimmy came waltzing up to our group full of joy and hope, telling us that he knew what we needed to do.

First, he had us gather up all the children in the tribe. We preached the Gospel to them and every single child gave their life to Jesus. We rejoiced over this victory, but knew that without getting the adults in the tribe saved, the children would not be able to hold onto their faith with much success. Without the guidance and support of the adults in the tribe, the children were being set up to fail in their walk with the Lord.

Second, Jimmy led us up onto a ridge that overlooked the area where the Tsataan lived. As we looked over the group of teepees below us, Jimmy told us about spiritual strongholds and what they were. He asked us what we thought the strongholds for this area were. We came up with shamanism, distrust, poverty, and other things that keep people from seeing Jesus as He is.

Jimmy then broke us up into groups of two and sent us along the ridge to pray over the Tsataan people. Jimmy told us that through our intercession we would bring spiritual breakthrough for the entire people group. I was skeptical whether this would work, but I was willing to try anything at this point.

We prayed our hearts out. After exerting all the faith that we had, we gathered as a group again. Jimmy said that we needed to thank the Lord for our victory and march around the Tsataan camp, like Jericho. We shouted, worshiped, and played guitars as loudly as we could. After we finished, nothing seemed to have changed to me, but Jimmy was sure something had happened.

We got word that there was another group of Tsataan people about five miles away. Jimmy sent a group of us to go tell them about Jesus. We saddled up and took off. Upon arrival, we told them about Jesus through a translator. They told us that they had heard about Jesus but hadn't chosen to follow Him.

A woman walked into the teepee; we were told she was the shamanist witch for the tribe. She could heal anyone of any disease, but the price she paid was extremely high. One of her children's lives was claimed each time she chose to heal a person. This woman was not evil. She wanted to help those around her and did so through the only means that she knew. The beauty of her heart was revealed through her willingness to endure horrible heartache to see others made well.

We told her that Jesus paid the price for our healing, and He was the only One who needed to die in order for healing to be effected upon a person. She invited us to pray for her, so we brought her outside the tent and laid hands on her. She began to sweat profusely as we prayed, even though it was cold enough to preserve snow outside. She said that she felt like fire was coursing through her body as we prayed.

After talking with the people a bit more about Jesus, we jumped on our horses and made our way back to camp.

As we rode up to camp my dear friend Elana was the first to notice that there was a definite difference in the atmosphere. Something about the spiritual realm felt distinctly lighter. We noticed that men were outside the teepees talking and laughing with each other. We had never seen these people even smile, let alone be social and enjoy each other. Something had changed. Was this what our prayers had done?

We got off our horses and talked to Jimmy about what we had observed. He immediately gathered a few people together and sent them into the chief's tent. They preached the Gospel in the exact same way that we had preached the first day we arrived at the tribe.

To our bewilderment, every person in the teepee gave their heart to the Lord, including the chief, who one day earlier had assured us that neither he nor any other adult in his tribe would follow Jesus. When the chief of a tribe makes a decision, the tribe follows in step. As a result, the entire tribe decided to give their lives to Jesus.

On the third day, just as the Lord had told Jimmy, we left the Tsataan people and started on our three-day journey back to the vans. We rode down the mountain, as the Reindeer people waved goodbye to us, now possessing a countenance of joy.

The local missionary who went with our group on this journey turned out to be specialized in discipling nomadic people. Scott ended up

making trips in the middle of winter to visit these people and disciple them. It was a full-meal deal!

A whole people group was brought into salvation to worship before the throne of God for all of eternity. This happened because one man decided to stay in faith, not waver in what God had told him, and press on until fruit manifested. Jimmy is my hero.

My Friend Rachel, Former Witch

Once, I stopped by Walmart to pick up an oil filter and oil. While at the purchasing counter, I looked over at the woman next to me and saw that in the middle of her forehead she had a tattoo of a pentagram with devil horns protruding out of it. My spirit man was sensing evil and an exceptional amount of pain coming from this woman's life and heart.

At that very moment the woman turned and started to stare at me. She asked me if she had met me before because she could have sworn that she knew me. I said that I had never met her before, but that her tattoo had caught my attention. She said she had taken vows to be a high priestess, and the tattoo was a result of the vows.

This was intriguing to me because for a few months the Lord had been stirring in me to pray against the satanic strongholds in my hometown,

which had been brought about by satanic worship. Now I found myself standing in front of a high witch who had been negatively influencing the spirit realm over my hometown for years. She was the very person I had been praying for whom God would dismantle with His love.

As Christians, we pray and intercede for revival, for unity within the Church, and for God to break the power of principalities over a region, but rarely do we think that we will be the ones to answer these prayers. The reality is that we do not pray to move God but to move us! God already wants to move. He is eager to bring His Kingdom. *We* are the ones who must be the brokers of Heaven. When we pray, God shapes us into the kind of people who become the answer to our prayers. This was Heaven's moment: A Spirit-filled lover of Jesus was talking to a high witch. Victory was unavoidable!

The woman shared that she was very upfront about her beliefs and that her intensity had been causing marital problems for her. Her husband was a Christian and her spirit worship had caused strife in their marriage because of the obvious differences between the two belief systems. She introduced herself, and I told her my name and shook her hand. To protect her, we will call her "Rachel."

I started speaking in tongues under my breath as I stood there, asking the Lord what He wanted to tell this woman. I was clueless about what to do, but I was sure of one thing: The Lord desires to love, save, and encourage all of His children. I wasn't going to leave until I had told her what He wanted to say to her.

The Father's voice started to resound in my spirit: "I love her, Tyler. I love her. She has endured so much pain. I love her." It was as though the Father was weeping over this woman in compassion and love.

I said, "OK, Lord, but what should I tell her?" He didn't answer my question, implying that all I needed in order to be effective in this situation was to have His heart for her.

I grew up learning how to minister lovingly, but not powerfully. Yet in the few years prior to this moment with Rachel, I had been learning that love without power is cruelty. Love without power lacks the ability to break the chains that hold God's children captive. It leaves people in bondage instead of freeing them. Put succinctly: If my love lacks power, it isn't truly love. *True love* is always powerful. An overwhelming sense of compassion was filling my heart for her, and I started to feel righteous anger toward all the things that had caused her pain over the years. Compassion always translated into power for Jesus, so I banked on it doing the same for me.

Still, I didn't know what to say, so I decided to stand there until something happened. One of the employees told me I could go to another department to ring up my item because Rachel's purchase was the only one they could process at the time. I told him that I would wait. He repeated himself, so I prayed that he would be quiet. I didn't want him to blow my cover; I was lying in wait to pounce on this hurting woman whom Jesus wanted to love. Surprisingly, the employee stopped trying to help me and left me standing there, still waiting. After five minutes or so, Rachel's purchase had gone through, and she started to make her way toward the door. I asked her if she would wait for me to buy my oil and filter because I wanted to talk with her more. She told me she would wait and would be outside by her car. I walked out a few minutes later, not knowing what I was going to say to her. She was out by her car with the hood popped and she was about to pour transmission fluid in.

I walked up to her car and said something stupid like, "Car work time, huh?" She asked me what I wanted to talk about. I said the first thing that came to mind, "I want to hear more about you and your husband."

She told me that recently her "mentor" had sat down to talk with her and her husband. The mentor told her husband, "Nobody will get between Rachel and the goddess. This means you." It was clear that Rachel was involved with a coven, and it was attempting to separate her from those who loved her.

I sensed it was time to share with her what was on my heart. I explained that while I was standing in line with her I had sensed a lot of pain in her life. I told her that I knew that she had gone through a lot of horrible things and that the things that had been done to her were wrong and unjust. I said that I was sorry that they had happened to her. She thanked me. Next, I told her that I believed she had a very good heart that wanted to help people. She nodded.

Rachel got out a few sticky notes and we exchanged cell phone numbers. I told her that if she ever needed help she could call me because I could pray for her. She asked me if I prayed to spirits for help. I told her, "Yes, I pray to a Spirit for help." Then she got very serious and asked me, "Do dead people communicate with you too?" She obviously received her spiritual power by consorting with the dead. I told her that I had been tempted to try to communicate with the dead in the past—because of my father's premature death and out of a deep ache of missing him—but I hadn't.

We were speaking the same language, though following very different gods. She felt safe to share things with me that are strange to the majority of North Americans because I validated the way that she perceived the world. The Bible sets forth an even more bizarre spirituality than that which the satanic church walks in: donkeys talking, seas parting, bones of a prophet raising people from the dead, handkerchiefs healing the sick, even people consulting the dead for advice and direction. The Bible makes it clear that these things happen, whether they are right

or wrong. When Rachel learned that I believed in things unseen, she started to trust me.

Hebrews 11 tells us that, *"Faith is…being certain of what we do not see."* If this is true (and it is), then witches, the satanic church, spiritualists, Buddhists, and New Age followers have more faith than most Christians.[1] That statement will severely mess up your theology. Meanwhile, most churchgoers are on the other end of the spectrum of faith. In general, most Christians are not only weirded out by just about *anything* unseen, like angels, demons, open heavens, the fire of God, portals, and glory clouds, but they even label manifestations like levitation as demonic and unredemptive in nature, despite the fact that Jesus did it (Mark 16:19).

She asked why I didn't talk with the dead. I told her because the Bible says not to—this was the first "Christian" word that I used. A shocked expression spread across her face, as though she wanted to take off sprinting. I said, "Whoa, wait a second. You are safe. Yeah, I am a Christian, but we are speaking the same language. Keep going." I could tell she was still uncomfortable, so I told her a second time that she was safe.

She asked, "You know the Holy Spirit then, don't you? That must have been what I sensed when I was standing next to you in line in the store. I felt positive energy coming from you." I smiled. She asked me, "Where do you go to church?" I told her that I went to a church in town. "Do they have the Spirit there?" she asked. I knew that my church didn't function on the level of spirituality that she was accustomed to, so I told

---

1. Please understand that I acknowledge that these religions follow the dark side of the unseen realm. Nonetheless, they believe in the unseen. Hebrews 11 doesn't clarify that it needs to be belief only in the good things in the unseen realm in order for it to be classified as faith.

her no. I could see from her perspective what it would take for people to be classified as "spiritual" people—people who use the prophetic and healing gifts regularly and as a way of life.

I asked her, "So you know about the Holy Spirit? Then what are you doing in this other religion?" She averted my question and asked me, "Why do you go to church if they don't have the Spirit?" I told her I went because I believed that the Holy Spirit could show up in any situation. She said, "Yeah, you are right."

Rachel then opened up and told me that many years back she had known the Holy Spirit and she used to go to church. She explained that because she was wired in a way that instinctively focuses on the spirit realm, she felt more understood, empowered, and able to use her gifts in a coven than in a church. I was simultaneously grieved and awed by this statement. She said, "If people aren't dancing, speaking in tongues, and interacting with the spirit realm, I can't enjoy it because it doesn't feel real to me. I need something that I can feel, something that I resonate with in my spirit."

The Bible is full of spiritual, supernatural events and people. You can open your Bible to just about any page and find something that is supernatural. The church hadn't been biblical enough for this witch.

The way Rachel was wired blew me away. She couldn't help but continuously function on a level of spirituality that most people in church never even step into. I don't agree with what she did (left the faith), but I can see why she did what she did, considering the way that she is wired.

She told me that she did want to help people, like I had told her. She was previously even involved in women's ministry, but now felt that through her "white magic" she was more able to help people than through the avenue of the church.

At this point I said that many people in Wicca, New Age, Spiritualism, Hinduism, Zen, and Buddhism are deceived in thinking that they can help people through "white magic." I told her quite bluntly that all "white magic" is the work of satan. She listened intently. I told her that God said we can only serve one god, and she wasn't serving the Lord anymore.

She received what I said. A trust had been established between us because I wasn't discounting her experiences and gifts like the church had. In fact, I was validating them. The way she was gifted wasn't unredemptive, it was wonderful. The issue was how she was using what she had.

I felt prompted to pray for her so I laid hands on her and started to pray. I sensed an internal battle in Rachel that I suspected was caused by the demons she had invited into herself through participating in different demonic practices. So I came against the darkness and bound it, then asked the Lord to give her peace so that she could receive what He wanted to say to her during that time. I prayed out a lot of things and I don't remember them all. The Lord had taken over, and I was acting more like an echo than speaking for myself. One thing I remember that He laid on my heart was His heart as a Father toward Rachel. I started to minister the Father's heart to her and speak about how He wanted to be her Father and wanted to heal the broken areas in her life caused by men. He had me pray about the lack and void left by her earthly father, and then I asked Him to fill those areas. I knew that I was free to pray in tongues over her because she was so open to the supernatural, so when what the Lord gave to my mind to pray ran out, I prayed out of my spirit to the Lord through tongues. It went on like this for a while.

Just as I was about to end the prayer, I felt a pain in my lower back. I asked Rachel if she had lower back pain and she said that she did. She said it had been especially bad lately. I asked her if I could place my hand on her lower back and she said that was OK. So I laid my hands on her

back and prayed that the Lord would heal her back and heal the areas of hurt in her emotional being that were related to the pain. I spoke life over her because she had had death spoken into her so many times over the past, and asked that the Lord would replace the death residing in her with life. I blessed her and asked for the Lord to come upon her and touch her.

When I ended the prayer, immediately Rachel started telling me that when she was 13 years old her father had died. She had always had a need for a father. She said that when I prayed for God to be her Father it had sealed the deal. I asked her what "sealed the deal" meant. She told me that three days prior, she had told her husband in a heated fight, "I cannot be with you anymore. The chasm that has opened up between us is too much for me to deal with. I cannot be with you anymore. I will never serve the Lord! But if the heavens open up and God makes it clear that He is speaking to me, I will go back to Him and we can be together again."

She said that my prayer had sealed the deal—she was now sure that God was speaking to her through me. She acknowledged that God was speaking to her because I knew that she had gone through so many hard things, because I had prayed about her need for a father, the accurate word of knowledge about her back, and because of the "positive energy" that she sensed when I was standing next to her in line at Walmart. She told me that when she saw me in Walmart she felt like she knew me and was drawn to what she sensed flowing from me. I was just standing there thinking about oil filters, but the Holy Ghost was reaching out, grabbing her with His love and power.

Rachel then opened up to a new extent and told me that I was right in saying that she had been through very hard things in life. She had been molested when she was child, had an abusive husband for years until she was finally forced to divorce him, participated in a homosexual relationship for years in reaction to her hatred toward men, and now

was in the midst of another broken marriage/relationship that had not fully fallen apart yet. It occurred to me that throughout her whole life she had been hurt and taken advantage of by men. It was amazing that she had allowed me to even talk to her, as well as to touch her when I laid hands on her to pray. I now realized why the Lord had me apologize to her on behalf of men. Because I am a man, the fact that I was sorry and recognized that what had been done to her was unjust spoke to areas deep within her that had needed to be validated for years.

I now had her attention and she could not deny that I was sent by the Lord to tell her what He wanted to say to her. I told her she needed to stop serving the enemy and come back to serve the Lord. She was starting to understand the fact that her "white magic" was the same as black magic or satanic worship, only disguised. I told her how satan loves to disguise himself as an angel of light, but is in fact the prince of darkness. She said, "Yes, I know you're right. I do call on the four corners for help, and I do see dead people, and they communicate with me. I guess that is proof that what I am following isn't all good." I almost laughed out loud in agreement with her statement.

Her next question was where she should go to church. I told her that I didn't know. At the time I didn't know about the churches in my town that are preaching the full Gospel, as Paul mentioned in Romans 15:19. I wish I had known about ministries like the Healing Rooms that follow a biblical perspective of the world.

Rachel had more than just a spiritual perspective on life; she had a biblical perspective. Hebrews 11:1 says that faith is believing in things unseen. Rachel believed in the unseen realm, while most Christians do not. Even in the midst of her idolatry, according to that verse, Rachel had more faith than most people who attend church. Our culture has a naturalistic view of the world, while the Bible incorporates both the spiritual realm and the natural realm into one paradigm. It is a grievance that the

majority of the Christians in North America are more influenced by our naturalistic culture than by the book that they pledge to believe.

At this point, the Lord started revealing to me the gifts Rachel had that she had been using to further the kingdom of darkness instead of the Kingdom of light. The Lord made it clear that He had wired her this way and with these giftings, but that they were being misused. He wanted me to communicate her gifts to her, mainly for the purpose of encouragement and affirmation, even if she already knew how she was gifted. I told her that she was very discerning and that I believed she also had a prophetic gift. She nodded and told me that when she walks into a crowded room she knows who is upset and why, who is happy, who is sad. In addition, she told me that she saw pictures of planes crashing into buildings two weeks before 9/11. This woman was so naturally gifted.

It was obvious to me that she had a huge inheritance in the Lord for a life of ministry. Rachel told me that she had always had a heart for Haiti and wanted to go there as a missionary. This seemed logical because the way that she would minister to people in Haiti would make sense to the people. They understand and function in the spiritual realm all the time, so her gifts would be heightened and appreciated by the people there.

I reminded Rachel that the inheritance the Lord had for her would not come about until she broke away from what she was presently following. I told her that it was clear that the Lord had an amazing life lined up for her of serving Him and people, but that it couldn't happen until she walked away from being a priestess.

Then I asked her, "You know where people worship satan in this area, don't you?" I asked this because two months prior, I had sensed that there was a lot of satanic worship going on in and around our hometown. In addition, a few days before that I had been driving in my car and at a specific spot in the road I had sensed evil all around me. I didn't know

what was going on out in the woods in that area, but I came to find out that other people also had felt uncomfortable in that particular area. Rachel told me the areas where the satanic rituals and worship took place and—lo and behold—it was the same area where I had felt uncomfortable as I was driving.

She asked me, "Did you get sick as you passed through that area?" I said, "Are you telling me that when these covens worship their demons, it releases the power to make people physically sick? Well, Jesus is bigger, more impressive, and more powerful than the devil, so nope, I didn't get sick. I worshiped—and the worship of Jesus draws Him to you and you to Him. When His Presence is present, no devil can overcome me. I worshiped because worship is a form of warfare and it pushes darkness away." Rachel took what I said to heart. I don't think she had ever been told to worship Him when she was scared of dark spiritual powers.

I told Rachel that in the name of Jesus she needed to break the vows she had made to satan. She said, "Yes, you're right. But I am scared. The women involved in my coven will come after me and I can already feel the fear rising up in me." I said, "You're right, they may come after you. But that is when you have to ground yourself in worship and the Word, and He will protect you. I want you to read Psalm 91 out loud every night. He will keep you safe. Satan mainly works through two ways: fear and intimidation. He will try to intimidate you and make you scared. But Jesus will protect you." She agreed to do so but was still shaken up. She said, "I just know it will be really hard when I lay my cloak and amulets down." I said, "You're right. It may be hard. But that is when you have to drape the cloak of Christ over you. In Ephesians 6 it talks about wearing the armor of God. You have to put it on. But you can't put it on until you have taken off the cloak that you are now wearing." Rachel knew what she needed to do. It was quite a decision. She was neck deep in being a high priestess, and for her to get out was a huge deal.

I told her to make the decision soon because the longer she waited, the harder it would become. To my surprise, she decided right then and there to give her life back to Jesus. It was an honor to witness the moment.

The next week I saw Rachel again. I found her and got to talk with her for a bit. She told me she is doing well. A few days after we first talked at Walmart, she packed up her car with all of her amulets, fetishes, scrolls, books, crystals, ceremonial items, and ritualistic clothes. She drove deep into to the woods and burned everything. She didn't sell all of that expensive stuff, she burned it. I was so proud of her. She said that her husband wasn't sure if her conversion was real or not until she did this.

Rachel told me she is doing well with standing her ground. Demons had been coming after her at night, but she told them, "I don't know who you are, but I am following Jesus now so you need to leave." Awesome.

We got a chance to pray together. She wanted to come to church. She asked me, "Do I need to wear nice clothes?" I told her, "Wear whatever you want. I usually wear something sort of nice." Then she asked, "Will people judge me for my tattoo?" I said "Probably, but that's OK. You will be with me. And my mom will love you up." She gave me a big hug and I drove off. She is following the Lord. She really is. It is a miracle. God won a high witch to Jesus.

Let Me Introduce the Holy Spirit

L ate one night I was working in the Night and Day prayer room at
the Healing Rooms, trying to clean and fix things. A car pulled by,
slammed on its brakes, and the passenger and the driver got out.
My friend Brett and a girl I had never seen before walked into the prayer
room and sat down as I continued to hammer nails down into the floor.
Brett and I started talking about God's power before I had a chance to
meet the girl he had brought with him. After a while our conversation
puttered out and he left the room to use the bathroom. I turned and faced
the girl.

I thought the girl knew the Lord, so I asked her how long she had
known Him. She told me that she didn't know Him. Kayla had stopped
being a Christian when she had been kicked out of church when she was
little for asking too many questions.

I stood up and immediately asked her for forgiveness on the behalf of Christians. I told her that my God is always merciful and good. I told her that the Christians who hurt her hadn't accurately represented the God I serve. My God is totally good, full of grace, forgiving, and always loving. And I told her that He loves her questions, even if they are rooted in doubt. He isn't threatened by her doubt.

I received a word about her writing and asked Kayla if she wrote. She said yes, poems. I told her God loved her poems, even if they weren't about Him. We were both so relaxed. After some time, I asked her what she was searching for, because I could feel that she was searching for something. I asked her what the longing of her heart was. I asked her if she still wanted God. She said she thought about Him all the time. Her hurt from other believers had marred her view of God, but she still knew in her heart who He was, and I could sense that. She didn't believe she had a relationship with God, but I suspected that was only because condemning, condescending, judgmental, hypocritical Christians had told her that.

She said, "I think about God all the time and try to talk to Him. But you guys talk about hearing from God or feeling Him, and I never do." I asked her, "Well, have you ever heard of the Holy Spirit?" She said no. I told her, "Well, the Holy Spirit is God on earth. He is who we feel and who we talk to. The reason you haven't felt like He hears you, why you don't feel like you can hear Him, and why you haven't felt His Presence is probably because nobody ever introduced you to Him." I asked her if I could pray for her, and she said yes. I started praying and I had a word about depression. The moment I broke that off, she started crying. I kept going, blessing her and releasing joy and peace over her. Then I got a word about shame, guilt, and condemnation. So I broke that off. Holy Spirit was in the room strongly at that point. I gave her a hug and kept praying.

I held Kayla's hands and led her in a prayer to receive the Lord. Then I had her pray, "Holy Spirit, come and fill me." But she didn't pray

it like that. In a loud, desperate, joyful shout, she prayed, "Holy Spirit, come and FILL ME!" It was wonderful. She was crying hard as the Holy Spirit filled her. I loosed more joy on her and she became filled with joy. Not laughter, but tears of joy. Smiles.

I asked her if she could feel Him now, and she said yes. She told me that she felt much better, as if she was lighter than before.

I told her that I didn't encourage people to go to the churches in town, but I do encourage people to go to the Healing Rooms. I gave her a hug goodbye, and she held on. There was pure, thankful, love there. She was a different girl!

About an hour later, I sent Brett a text with my mobile phone. He was just dropping Kayla off at home because she needed to have some time to cry in private. She hadn't stopped crying tears of joy and thankfulness since she had left the prayer room.

So once again, by the use of the prophetic, another person came to Jesus.

Jesus at the Airport

I am learning that it is *right* to bring someone to a place where they have to make a decision about Jesus. Not forcefully of course, but if people aren't given a clear choice, then they can't clearly choose Jesus. In the same manner, a person can't choose to not go to hell if you don't give then a choice *not* to go there. Whenever I have simply asked people if they want to follow Jesus, they have always said yes. I just need to merely ask more. The story of Jesus at the airport is a perfect example.

God loves to move on people in the least churchlike places, like the airport. I was in an airport on my way home from fishing in Alaska. I started talking to a Hispanic guy from California named Jesus who had been working in a cannery. He had a rash on his back from the fish. I nonchalantly told him that Jesus wanted to heal him and didn't want him to have a rash anymore. He sounded intrigued by my comment, so I asked him if I could pray for his healing.

This was the first time I learned how to release the Holy Spirit on people in faith. If you operate in faith, He will move every time. I prayed a simple prayer, rebuked and cursed the rash, blessed him, loosed Holy Spirit on him, and said amen.

When I finished, I opened my eyes to see that this man was weeping. Tears were splashing onto the tile floor. He thanked me, then just sat there crying. After some time, I asked him what he was feeling. He said that he felt something like relaxation taking place deep down. I love the nonreligious language that unbelievers use when they experience God. I said, "Oh, that is Jesus. It is His peace."

After a few moments of silence, I asked him if he knew Jesus. He said that he didn't. Then I simply asked him if he wanted to. He said, "Yeah, I don't know why not."

I led him in a prayer and he started weeping again, filled with the love and peace of Jesus. I didn't say anything profound; it was completely God's Presence that caused him to weep. After we were done praying he hugged me over and over again in gratitude. I felt so loved.

We talked for the next few hours about how to read the Bible and pray. It was such a beautiful time. He was such a receiver. I was able to give him a book and some food, and we spent a few of the most beautiful hours together that I had experienced in a long time.

Then we started talking with another fisherman sitting nearby, and it turned out that he was already in love with Jesus. Before we knew it, he started giving the testimony of how he got saved. Jesus piped in as soon as the fisherman was done, and boldly started telling about his recent experience with the Lord. They were talking exceptionally loud in a little room with about 25 fishermen and crabbers within earshot. Those rough fishermen clearly heard about God's love that day, and there was nothing they could do about it. It was great.

We ended up flying to the next city, where the three of us talked and ate together in the airport until our next flights. It was a God thing. We were all so encouraged.

A Small World

Though this story doesn't involve an overt conversion, it does possess a peculiar amount of "coincidence." My wife and I were living in Redding at the time, attending Bethel's Supernatural School of Ministry.

I was jogging on my way to a nearby gym to work out. As I ran along the sidewalk of a busy street, I came upon a group of police cars and ambulances in the road. I looked past their flashing lights to see a young girl, probably 16 years old, lying in the street. She had been hit by a car. I started asking the Lord what I should do and how to go about releasing the Kingdom. I looked and saw four other Bethel students standing on the other side of the road, also looking at the girl. God had brought five Holy Ghost-filled believers to be there to comfort this girl when she was in such a scary situation.

I didn't know what was wrong with her, but right in the middle of the road the paramedics started putting the girl in a brace. We released peace and healing over her and talked to her long enough to find out that she didn't know Jesus before the ambulance whisked her away. We grabbed her stuff, which was strewn across the road, and went to the hospital so that we could love on her and give her belongings back to her. When we got there, we were told that we couldn't see her. We left her stuff at the front desk and went home.

Two days later I went to go work out again. Just as I was getting through with my workout, I saw an Indian woman who caught my eye. We ended up in a conversation, and very quickly she started opening up about her life. Early on in our conversation, without me talking about God in any way, she said, "I know religion is a very private thing, but I have a lot of questions about life and I need to find the answers to my questions." That was like loading a gun and then handing it to me. She set me up!

It turned out that she worked in the ER and saw a lot of horrible things each day, and it had finally gotten to her. She recognized that horrible things could come upon a morally good person as easily as a person who is incredibly immoral. And because she believed in karma, she was confused at the contradiction of the two. One question she had was, "Why did those ten people's houses burn down and those five's didn't?" She was thinking along these lines.

I told her that I didn't know the answers to the suffering in the world, but that Jesus' love and peace kept me in a place where I didn't need to know the answers. I told her that His love and peace made *me* the answer to the situations around me that were wrong, sad, and hard.

I ended up praying for her and releasing the Holy Spirit over her. I didn't say much...I just asked Him to come. When previously in my walk with the Lord it was unfathomable for me to expect for Him to show

up when I pray, I now have the faith to know that when I ask for Him to come, He will. He did come as we started to pray, and she started crying. Literally, I had nothing to say in the prayer, so I just invited Him. My words had nothing to do with it. What was in the air was everything. Presence evangelism works really well. People thirst for the peace and warmth that God's Presence brings to their spirit. People in North America are much more spiritual than we think.

Then the Presence lifted, and I loved on her a bit. We talked some more, but she wasn't hearing much truth, so I prayed for her again. The same thing happened again: She started crying as His Presence came. I asked her if she knew Jesus and she told me that she didn't. I was going to ask her if she wanted to receive His love into her heart, but I couldn't get a word in. She spoke extremely fast, without periods, commas, or spaces.

The coincidental part of this story is that she told me that the primary thing that led her to asking these questions about God was that two days prior she had seen a girl come into the ER who had been hit by a car. The girl asked the Indian woman to pray for her, because before she had arrived people had been praying for her and it had helped immensely. This woman didn't know how to pray for her. All she could do to help was hold her hand for 30 minutes. The woman was shaken up by it. She realized that her patients need something more than what she currently possessed. It made her desperate. I asked her the girl's name, and it was the same girl whom we had prayed for two days prior in the middle of the street.

I blessed her and left.

Déjà Vu

A week before I was scheduled to train a group of hungry church leaders, my wife had a dream about my upcoming time with them. My wife described that in the dream someone was born again while I was with this group. The entire group erupted in rejoicing, and the dream abruptly ended. This was a peculiar dream in my opinion, because I knew that every person who would be at this retreat had already come into a personal relationship with Jesus.

On the closing night of the conference, the group was eating dinner as they asked my spiritual father and me questions about the healing ministry. Five minutes into dinner, two young men walked into the large dining room. They seemed to be confused, as if they were in the wrong place. But I knew they were in the right place because of the dream. I quickly ushered them down the line of food with a plate in their hands,

dumping food onto their plates. I pulled a table off the wall and set up chairs for them, placing brownies and other desserts on the table for them. They seated themselves hesitatingly, as I reassured them that we wanted them to eat their fill.

As I sat at their table and talked with them, another young man in the room clued in to the fact that these two men needed Jesus. With a loud voice, he asked, "Why does God send people to hell?"

The room fell silent and everyone looked at me. I stood from the small table where I was sitting a little ways from the main tables where the group sat. The eyes of these two men watched me closely as I explained to the group that God does not send anyone to hell, but that He desires for none to perish. With a consciousness that I was really speaking to our two visitors, I preached my heart out about hell to the main group. I didn't do so in an old-fashioned, fire and brimstone repentance message, but by explaining that a person sends himself to hell when he rejects God's free gift of love through Jesus. I explained that there is no logical reason why any person should perish because the Gospel is truly good news. Eternity in Heaven, the greatest gift anyone could receive, is free. If that isn't good news, I said, I don't know what is.

I preached about God's love, but I preached it with a conviction that hell is a real place. I don't dwell upon the reality of hell for the sake of preaching about it to the unbeliever, but for my own sake. See, while a revelation of Heaven makes us yearn for Jesus, a revelation of hell gives us a yearning to save souls. I want to know the reality of hell so that I am motivated to go out and tell others about God's love. Without a conviction that people who don't have Jesus will go to hell, I won't go out of my way to convince others, even beg them if necessary, to receive Jesus.

The Holy Spirit started to rest upon the people in the room as I told a story about a relative of mine who visited hell when his heart surgery went awry. He had been a lukewarm believer his entire life, banking

on his wife's faith. During this surgery he suddenly found himself in hell. What struck him most about the experience was that he couldn't get out of the place. He was stuck in this prison of astonishing horrors. After a short time, a Being of Light came to him and pulled him out of this dreadful place, and he woke up in the hospital, absolutely hysterical. You would think that a person just pulled out of hell would be peaceful or at least relieved, but hell is such a destructive, horrifying place that it takes time to recover from the experience. In the meantime, he was hysterical. Since his experience at the hospital, he has been a different man. He now spends time with Jesus daily and his children and wife attest to an obvious difference in him.

Toward the end of the story about my relative, the Spirit was thick in the room. I told everyone in the room to close their eyes. I asked anyone who wanted to be born again to raise their hands. Both of the young men raised their hands and then prayed to receive Jesus and be born again.

These two men were in good company. The majority of the people present were involved in the Healing Rooms, so naturally these men got a lot of prayer and many prophetic words. Soon tears were starting to creep from the corners of their eyes as people nailed prophetic words about their lives. After prayer they told us that they were brothers, and one of them mentioned that he had a shoulder problem that kept him from being able to raise his arm well or pick up his children. We prayed for his healing, then invited them to stay for the next session, which I was speaking at. They excitedly stayed.

I spoke on intimacy with Jesus and took people on an encounter to Heaven. We can't just talk about God, we must experience Him. Afterward I asked people to raise their hands if they had encountered God in a vision. One of the brothers raised his hand high in the air, but kept it raised long after everyone else had put their hands down. I began laughing

as I realized that his arm being raised high in the air was communicating to everyone that he had not only seen Jesus in a vision, but that his shoulder had been healed.

God gave this man a full-meal deal. He had committed his life to Christ, received eternity in Heaven, been filled with the Spirit, been healed, and even had a vision of Jesus. Yet without the dream I would never have leaned into what God wanted to do that night. I am thankful to have a wife who hears from God.

God has an agenda, but we rarely lean into what He wants to do because we aren't listening. I sadly find myself living by my own agenda instead of living by the Voice in the present tense. Part of the fallen nature of man is to live by programs and regularities rather than by God's voice. Without our partnership, God still does good things, but for wonderful things to happen we need to be listening. We can settle for the good, or we can have the best.

From Bars to Heaven

I was in the Night and Day Prayer Room for my midnight to 2:00 A.M. prayer shift. I saw a picture of a young man wearing a black coat standing outside of a local bar in town, which I recognized as being down the street from the prayer room. The Lord said, "If someone merely tells this man, 'You need Jesus,' he will give his life to Me."

I got up and walked out of the prayer room onto the rain-soaked street. As the rain misted down upon me, I crossed the road, walked over to the bar that I had seen in the vision, and leaned against the cold building to watch for a man with a black coat.

Though it was late, the alcohol scene was just warming up. People were getting in fights, others were smoking their cancer sticks, and some were in groups outside the bar talking. I looked intently for a man with a black coat but couldn't spot one.

After about ten minutes of watching for my divine appointment, I started planning my return to the prayer room. I was considerably wet at this point. As I was about to leave, I noticed a young man wearing a black coat walk out of the bar with a woman. He fit the description of the man in the vision, and I happened to know the woman he was with. I walked up to the two of them and said hello to the woman who I knew from high school. She asked me what I was doing standing outside the bar in the rain. I told her that I had been in prayer and that God had told me about a young man wearing a black coat down at the bar. They were both very interested by this. I pointed to him and highlighted the fact that out of all of the people outside he was the only one with a black coat on.

I looked at this man and point blank asked him, "You need Jesus, don't you?" His head dropped and he quietly responded in a whisper, "Yes, I do."

I told them about the prayer room and invited them to come with me to pray for a while. They accepted my invitation and followed me across the puddle-filled parking lot to the building where the prayer room was.

We entered the prayer room and I started playing some worship music on the CD player. I wanted His Presence to lead them into salvation, not my words. We sat in quiet prayer for some time. After I felt peace in the room, I started talking to the young man about his life. My friend from high school also shared about her life. They were dissatisfied with the condition of their lives, to say the least.

The woman ended up rededicating her life to the Lord that night. The young man admitted that he needed God and that his life was falling apart without Him. God's love washed over them as we prayed together, and they left very different people.

The bar no longer seemed to appeal to them. Though the bar was still open when they left the prayer room, they got into their cars and drove home. Nothing the earth can offer is as pleasurable as God's love, and that night they had drank deeply of it through our time together.

Revival and Resurrection Power

…We are rinthian*more than conquerors through Him who loved us.*
(Romans 8:37)

*Heal the sick, raise the dead, cleanse those who have leprosy,
drive out demons. Freely you have received, freely give.*
(Matthew 10:8)

And for those who think the above verse
was only a command given to the apostles:
*Therefore go and make disciples of all nations…teaching
them to obey* **everything** *I commanded you…*
(Matthew 28:19-20)

*Now if Christ is preached, that He has been raised from the dead,
how do some among you say that there is no resurrection of the
dead? But if there is no resurrection of the dead, not even Christ
has been raised; and if Christ has not been raised, then our
preaching is vain, your faith also is vain. Moreover we are even
found to be false witnesses of God, because we testified against
God that He raised Christ, whom He did not raise, if in fact the
dead are not raised. For if the dead are not raised, not even Christ
has been raised; and if Christ has not been raised, your faith is
worthless; you are still in your sins.*
(1 Cos 15:12-17 NASB)

*Why should any of you consider it incredible
that God raises the dead?*
(Acts 26:8)

The Parking Lot Revival

My friend Adam and I had driven to a conference in Redding, California. On the closing night, we both were touched by God in a significant way.

When the speaker laid his hands on me for impartation, I was filled with power. I was literally thrown through a partitioning wall by the force of what he imparted. When I got off the ground my body was involuntarily shaking. I felt like someone had sat me down at a bar and pumped a whole keg into my mouth in a matter of 30 seconds. The room was spinning, but I didn't feel out of control. I felt great.

I tripped my way back to my seat, enjoying the bliss that I was experiencing. I desired to give it to Adam just as the minister had given it to me. Freely I received, so freely I wanted to give it away. I prayed over Adam and nothing happened. I couldn't figure out why nothing happened when I could feel power surging through my body.

We walked out into the parking lot and I decided that I was going to give to Adam what I had just got, no matter what I had to do to release it. He is my best friend and an amazing minister of the Gospel. He needed this impartation in order to do what God had called him to do with the lost. It wasn't OK that it hadn't yet dropped into his lap like it did for me.

I told him to prepare himself, because I was going to give this impartation to him no matter what it took. He agreed, so I charged him and tackled him in prayer.

I guess it worked, because Adam started acting really odd. He began laughing, hunched over, and backed up into some trees and street signs. Someone in the parking lot saw this and came over to see what we were doing. This man discerned that Adam and I had been touched by the Lord, and brought a group of about a dozen people over for Adam and me to pray for.

Adam and I started laying hands on the people in the group, and the same thing that had happened to Adam and I started to happen to every person in the group whom we laid hands on. It looked different for every person. People were all over the ground, some screaming, some worshiping, some laughing, some trying to get up under the weight of God's glory.

At that time in my life, what I thought it looked like when people experienced God was severely limited. But I couldn't deny what I was witnessing: It was obvious that people were experiencing God. It didn't look like what I was accustomed to, but people were clearly enjoying the Holy Spirit and connecting with the Lord through it. Who was I to take that connection away from them by judging what was happening?

We were quite the sight, and as a result more people began to walk up to our group, wondering what was going on. Adam could no longer

get off the ground to pray for people, so I would either lay hands on a person myself or pick Adam up like a bag of potatoes and stick his hand on their head. Every time we laid hands on people they fell over. We never told them that falling over was the norm and we never pushed them. In fact, we would barely touch them. It was totally God's doing.

By this time the group had swelled to over 100 people. People started pulling up their cars and cranking worship music so that everyone could hear it. Worshipers danced with flags all over the parking lot. Some sections broke out their guitars and started to worship in their own group. Adam was still on the ground. He kept repeating, "I can't get up, man," between bouts of laughter. I circled the group, looking for people who needed a dose of the Ghost.

It became really fun laying hands on people, praying "fire" over people, and watching the Holy Spirit tackle them like I did Adam.

What astonished me was that unbelievers started showing up, who had never before seen the manifestations of the Holy Spirit. They walked up to me and said, "I want what they have." I just laid my hand on their heads and said, "Take it! It is free! FIRE!" They fell over, and I just left them there on the cold ground. They got up a few minutes later as new people. People were saved in this irregular way that night. The Presence of God is a great avenue for evangelism.

Eventually, this small revival grew to around 200 people. People pulled into the parking lot while others, who had received their fill, pulled out. We just kept going. I realized that this outpouring would continue as long as we had new people to give it away to. All outpourings work off the same basic principle. As long as you keep giving it away, God will keep giving it to you.

A camera crew even showed up. They started taping what was happening and interviewing people who were laid out on the cold ground. And I didn't hear one person complain that the ground was cold.

People were healed as well. I know of a knee that was healed that night, but another man's miracle was even more interesting. A Hispanic man walked up to me and said, "I am missing a testicle and I want it back." To such a bold request I simply said, "OK!" He told me that it grew back as I was praying. I took his word for it. No need for visual confirmation, please.

After three hours of God madness, the glory lifted when there were no more new people to give it to. So we left.

People had experienced God, bodies had been healed, and unbelievers had stumbled upon God's glory and had been saved. I heard from a few of them that they just felt drawn to drive to the parking lot where we were.

The next day we left to drive back home to the Northwest. As we were leaving, Adam received the number *154* and saw an odd picture of a man with plugs in his ears. Knowing how to interpret words of knowledge, Adam quickly deduced that the man he saw in the vision was probably deaf. He told me about it, and asked me if I thought we would find the man on exit 154 off of the I-5 freeway. I told him that I didn't know, but I was open to try.

We had about six other people with us in the car, and the exit was hundreds of miles away. Home was even further down the road. It was quite a risk for Adam to ask the entire group of people to pull off the freeway for him after hours of driving. They wanted to get home and rest, but out of sheer pity they decided to pull off the highway at exit 154.

Exit 154 was the least likely place for a deaf man to be, let alone any people at all. The exit led us onto a country road without many buildings. There wasn't a soul in sight. At this point, a few people in the car started to get a bit irritated with Adam and aggressively asked him, "Well, where do we go now?" Adam didn't know. He calmly explained that God

had only given him the exit and the picture of the man. I admired him for not feeling like he needed to have the answer. This wasn't his doing in the first place, and he could only be held accountable for what he was given. In not giving an answer, Adam made himself vulnerable to everyone else's criticism. But he held his own and quietly trusted the Lord with a steady faith.

We aimlessly drove down country roads, turning here and there. We had no idea where to go. Suddenly we came to a house. We briefly stopped to look at the house, and Adam jumped out of the car. Boldly, he went right up to the front door and knocked on it.

A woman came to the door, and Adam asked if by any chance there was a deaf man who lived there. She said yes.

God had told Adam about a person in *another state* who needed prayer for healing. We found out later that this man was the only deaf man in that whole county. The woman who answered the door was not shocked when Adam asked her if a deaf man lived there because she didn't know that we didn't know *anything* about them.

We ended up praying for the man to be healed. The family had a hard time believing that God *wanted* to heal him. They would not believe that we knew about the man's deafness because God had told Adam. Their unbelief caused them to assume that we had found out about the man's deafness through natural means. They figured that we had stopped down the road and found out about the man's handicap from someone in the area. They didn't trust us, though we had no agenda but to see this man healed. Fear seemed to plague their household, so we released God's love the best we knew how, prayed for him, and started to get back into the car to leave.

One of the younger boys in the family started talking to me as our group was getting into the car. It turned out that he already had a bad

knee at the age of 12. I prayed for it and the pain instantly left. He was impressed by that, and rededicated his life to the Lord on the spot as a result. I wish the rest of the family would have had the receptive heart that little Danny did. God was ready to show off if they had let Him.

A few days after we returned home, we received an audio clip from one of the women who had been with us. She had attached a microphone to her MP3 player and put it in her pocket, which she accidentally turned on during the outpouring in the parking lot. It ended up that she had recorded around ten minutes of the holy mayhem. It sounded like utter chaos: random singing, odd sounds, screaming, and loud rejoicing. The noises that came from that clip made me somewhat uncomfortable, even though I was there and witnessed that nothing harmful or ungodly was happening. Though my natural mind was somewhat put off by the recording for the first few times I listened to it, every time I played the clip, the Presence of God would rest on me in the most delightful way.

God will speak however He finds fit. Adam had the wisdom to trust that God was speaking to him, and obediently followed the Lord in detail. In doing so, we witnessed one of the most powerful words of knowledge that I have ever seen.

God will also come in any way that He chooses. We pray for revival, but when it comes we often disregard it to be emotionalism and fanaticism, or worse, demonic. Revival will probably never come as we expect it to. Jesus embodied a spirit of revival. The spiritual leaders of His day totally missed the Move of God because He didn't come in the way they expected. Inherent in a spirit of revival is a line of demarcation. A move of God that doesn't have critics is not a move of God. God will never send something to earth that is palatable to every believer. He does this to separate and divide those who are hungry and pure in heart from those who are just religious and wearing a mask of righteousness.

God will show up however He pleases, even in bodies laid out in a cold parking lot, odd pictures, and exit numbers. When the Upper Room emptied out, people were so unaccustomed to God's people being filled with joy and freedom that they thought they were drunk on alcohol. God will show up in any way that He wants to, but especially in a way that is outside our box. Lose your box.

The Dead Raising Team

After witnessing people being healed and delivered, I began to seek God for opportunities to completely obey His commandment in Matthew 10:8, *"Heal the sick, cleanse the lepers, raise the dead, and cast out devils"* (KJV). While people had been healed and delivered, I had yet to lay my hands on a dead body and have it raised to life. To my way of thinking, I was not only missing out on experiencing another aspect of God's power and goodness, but I wasn't fully obeying God.

A passion to see God's will manifested pertaining to dead raising began to burn in me like a bonfire. This fire caused me to fervently seek God in prayer asking Him to make a way for me to have an opportunity to pray for the dead. I realized that if I was going to see the dead raised I needed to go *find* dead people. The dead aren't like the sick: They will not waltz into your church or ministry and ask for prayer to be made better.

If I was going to obey God, that meant I had to go out of my way to find people who had died. The whole idea of touching a dead body was unnerving to me, but I wanted to do what Jesus said we could, would, and should do.

Consequently, I wrote a letter to the owner of our local funeral home. In the letter I shared my desire that no one would lose his or her loved ones to premature death. I told him that God raises the dead today, and then asked the director to allow me to pray for the dead if the family of the deceased agreed to it.

Not surprisingly, I didn't get a response back from the funeral director. I wrote and sent the letter presupposing that he would think I was crazy.

I knew that I would most likely get some backlash for stepping outside the box of the Christian majority, but sometimes the desire to see God be God causes one to fling oneself into the controversial, like a person walking into oncoming traffic. I didn't care what opposition came in my direction, I had to see the dead raised.

Opposition came—not from nonbelievers but from religious Christians. No surprise there: The people who most opposed Jesus and Paul were the religious. These people professed to follow God yet had no problem with killing God on earth (Jesus). People are a bit confused when they oppose God and yet profess to follow Him. In doing so, they reveal their lack of knowing and recognizing Him.

During those days I learned to continue to walk toward the Prize regardless of who was trying to ruin my life or discourage me from what God was telling me to do. God quickly distanced me from these people so that He could continue to do through me what He wanted to do.

It became clear to me that by our words, judgments, and thoughts, we determine how high others can go in God. Others can go as far in God

as we allow them to. If we struggle with their passion, calling, and victories and do not rejoice with them when they experience victory or blessings, God will distance us from them so that they are not held back in what He has set before them to do. God does not like glass ceilings.

Likewise, if you have people in your life who are quick to assume that what God is doing in your life comes from the enemy, they have stepped onto very thin ice with God pertaining to their relationship with you. God will not allow His plan for your life to be hindered by their judgments, lack of encouragement, and jealousy.

God is quick to move when the Holy Spirit is being blasphemed (see Mark 3:22-29). Blasphemy of the Holy Spirit is when we label that which is of God as that which is of the enemy, and it is a very serious sin in God's eyes. Jesus even told us that it is the one sin that is unforgivable, which should carry some weight pertaining to the seriousness of this topic. It is not an unforgivable sin because God will not forgive it, but because the person who makes this type of judgment is so sure about their assumption that they refuse to change their mind. Therefore, they do not *want* to be forgiven. We should be very careful not to jump to conclusions about what is God and what isn't God.

Shockingly, two months after I had written and sent the letter to the funeral home director, his son was killed in a car accident.

When I arrived at the funeral home to visit the family and talk to the funeral director I said, "You know why I am here and what my motive is in coming. I am so sorry for what has happened. Do I have your permission to pray for his resurrection?" He looked at me with tears streaming down his face and said, "Tyler, get him back. Get him back."

For the next four days I prayed harder than I ever had before. I did my best. I went to the funeral home in the evening, waited until the last visitor left, then prayed throughout the night until morning broke on the

horizon. I fasted, asked every person I knew who moved in power to pray, prayed in tongues for days, read and prayed every verse on dead raising over and over, and worshiped like a drug addict who had just been saved.

Though the young man wasn't raised, in those four days I learned about my authority to raise the dead. After what many would call a failure, I was stronger in my conviction, faith, and passion about resurrection power. Defeat can either make you give up or it can make you rise to the call of victory. I was now all the more sure that the next time I got a chance to raise the dead, the dead would be raised.

Because of this new boldness that God gave me, I started approaching fatal car accidents whenever I saw them. When I spotted an accident as we were passing on the highway, instead of praying for the person being hauled away to the ambulance from the safe confines of my car, I jumped out to see if I could pray for them.

Once, less than a mile from our house, a woman plowed into a semi-truck head on. She was killed instantly. I sprinted to the scene and stood behind the irritating yellow tape that had been strung up by the police to keep curious bystanders from getting in the way. I told the nearby policeman that I was a chaplain and minister of the Gospel, and that I had authority to raise the woman from the dead. Unsurprisingly, he looked at me like I was nuts, his face not unlike what I imagine the funeral home director's expression looked like when he read my letter. The police officer glanced at my ordination and chaplain cards, and radioed in asking if I could cross the tape. I was surprised he even did that. He told me that they already had a chaplain on scene, so I wasn't needed. I thought to myself, *Yeah, but that chaplain isn't going to try to pray for resurrection. That is the difference.*

After a few attempts in this manner at car accidents, the director of Emergency Services in our county caught wind of what I was doing. One night he came to me and simply said, "I heard you have been

approaching car accidents in an attempt to raise the dead, but you are having a hard time crossing the police line."

I didn't know what he was getting at. My first thought was that I might be in trouble. I swallowed deeply, then I told him that he had heard right. Making a statement that surprised me, he humbly replied, "Would you like to do it with the authority of the state behind you?"

A week later I met this man of God in his office, where he quietly issued me a laminated card with my picture on it enabling me to access any accident scene without being stopped by the police. If more planes are flown into buildings, I will be able to be at ground zero to help. I was grateful, to say the least. God was making a way.

A week later, I found myself on a country road, stuck in a traffic jam. It was either roadwork taking place at noon (which was unlikely) or it was a car accident. I decided to find out the actual authority that the card carried, so I jumped out of the car and ran down the side of the road toward the cause of the traffic jam. I rounded a bend in the road to see that a car had slid off the road and there were cops swarming around, keeping onlookers behind the frustrating yellow tape. I flashed my card, and sure enough, I was suddenly ushered past the tape and right into the mix of the accident. Nobody was harmed in the accident so I headed back to my car, thoroughly pleased.

We soon gathered a loosely associated group of people across the state of Washington who were like-minded in praying for the dead to be raised. A friend of mine named Mike even met up with the chief coroner over his county and found favor with him. We called each other for support when we were about to go pray for the dead, and we constantly encouraged each other to believe God for a full release of power over our lives. I had some cards printed out stating what we did and the service we offered, and I asked the local funeral home if they would display the cards for families that had just lost a loved one to pick up. Because of our

sensitivity in the previous situation with the funeral director's son, they eagerly displayed our cards. We were soon labeled the "DRT"—the Dead Raising Team—though we had never actually raised the dead. God loves to call that which isn't yet as though it is.

Then our success happened. A dear friend of mine who was a part of our loosely associated group of like-minded people had a breakthrough.

Marsha and her son were attending revival meetings during an outpouring of the Spirit. After a few days attending the meetings, Marsha and her son began driving to the coast in hopes of relaxing at the beach.

Meanwhile, a young man was paddling out into the ocean on his surfboard from the very same beach where Marsha and her son were headed to relax. While this man was on the water something must have gone terribly wrong, because he ended up drowning in the ocean. After dragging his lifeless body out of the water, the lifeguards did their best to resuscitate him. Though they were trained in CPR and other life-saving education, they could not get a heartbeat. Once they had thoroughly given their best effort to bring him back, the man was pronounced dead. The ambulance was called to take his body to the hospital morgue.

Enter Marsha and her son. Marsha walked up to the scene, told the lifeguards that she was a minister who healed people, and began praying in the Spirit, as did her son. When this heavenly language started to spill from her mouth, people nearby began to mock her, but Marsha boldly and courageously continued.

After five minutes or so, she opened her eyes to find that while the mocking was still continuing, other believers had joined her in prayer, standing beside her in agreement. The moment she realized that others had joined them, Marsha's faith increased exponentially. At that moment, life entered the young man again and he was raised to life. When they finally finished praying, the young man was without brain damage and

was able to move all parts of his body, completely restored from death! That day he and everyone standing nearby had a fresh revelation of Jesus' love and power.

Marsha's success became our success. We believed for years that it could happen, and God had finally done it. Since I got the card and Marsha had victory over death, we have had other breakthroughs in raising the dead. A baby has resurrected in the womb, and other miracles have taken place in hospitals. We have seen elderly people that were on their deathbed in the Intensive Care Unit, now living. In the Kingdom, the young live to be old and the old live to be older.

We strongly believe that this level of power is only the beginning. We believe that the Church will walk in such power that She will be clearing out morgues and emptying funeral homes in the name of Jesus.

Because of the testimony of God's power, people from different places in the United States have called us asking for advice on how to start their own DRT. Many people already have groups assembled and are ready to raise those whom the enemy steals from them through sickness and premature death. They are modern day Minutemen, filled with the power of God and far more courageous than the Minutemen of history that fought natural wars. I am encouraged by the desire of those in America who hear the call from Heaven to raise the dead according to Jesus' command in Matthew 10:8. They are refusing dry, dead, religious Christianity, and are walking in life-giving, tangibly powerful friendship with God. The result is Heaven on earth.

We are the answer to the world's problems because we contain God. God is in us! This is fabulous—and it's the only plan God has to save the lost. There is no Plan B. Death and disease afflict humanity daily, bringing injustice upon the lives of those who are created in God's image. If we do not become the solution to the world's pain and problems, who will?

Visions of Intimacy

…I will pour out My Spirit on all people.
Your sons and daughters will prophesy,
your young men will see visions…
(Acts 2:17)

And God raised us up with Christ and seated
us with Him in the heavenly realms in Christ Jesus.
(Ephesians 2:6)

You have stolen my heart, my sister, my bride;
you have stolen my heart
with one glance of your eyes…
(Song of Songs 4:9)

"Teacher, which is the greatest commandment in the Law?"
Jesus replied: "'Love the Lord your God with all
your heart and with all your soul and with all
your mind.' This is the first and greatest commandment."
(Matthew 22:36-38)

The Greatest Commandment Precedes the Great Commission

Like salvation, healing, and anything else in the Kingdom, visions are accessed by faith. This vision happened while I was in quiet prayer, as is true with all the visions in this section.

I saw myself standing next to the Father as a child. I was holding His hand, but reluctantly. I watched myself attempt to break free from His loving grip and run to the lost in order to tell them about Him, but He wasn't letting me go yet. Our arms were taut as I continued the violent pulling on His arm. After enough time of tiring myself out, I finally relented and stood at His side unwillingly, like a child put in time-out.

But over time I started to like Him. I started to relax my hand. I began to hold His hand instead of trying to squirm out of His kind grip.

Soon I was looking at His big hand, caught in the wonder of His strength. I found myself adoring Him. No longer was I holding His hand with only one hand, but both of mine firmly grasped His. I was learning how lovely He was.

With the beginning stages of my love for Him being established, His big hand suddenly opened and released me. I looked up at Him with an astonished face, like that of a child who is finally allowed to do something he wanted to do for years but was never old enough to do until that moment. He smiled, and I took off running. The lost gave me so much life because I saw Jesus in them, so I ran straight in their direction.

Then I could no longer see from my viewpoint, but I began to see from the Father's. I watched myself run straight into a pack of wolves. And we were both OK with that. He sends us out like sheep among wolves.

God desires a relationship with you before sending you out to do ministry. He knows that you won't be able to minister to others until He has ministered to you, so He sets this divine order to your life. Be loved, as your name suggests (the Beloved), and only then, go.

Life Through Death

I was at an enormous table of food with Jesus. As He looked across the table and into my eyes, He held up a wine glass as if wanting to make a toast. I told Him that I wanted to go to the chambers with Him (Song of Songs 1:4), but He communicated that I needed to eat. I took my eyes off of His Beauty, and looked at the table to see food of every kind spread out before me.

He handed me some bread and I knew without Him saying anything that it was the Bread of the Presence, which represented God's daily provision. He told me to eat of it. In doing so, I ate of His body.

Then He asked me if I could drink the cup that He held out over the table. He didn't *tell* me to drink it or ask me if I *would*, but if I *could*. I didn't know if I could, because I knew that the cup represented the bitterness and suffering of Jesus. The cup is death to self, and Jesus drank it

to a fatal degree. But the cup is also the sweetness of His glory and life abundant. Though there is suffering, there is incomparable life and joy in the midst of it. I drank.

Therefore we made a covenant together, to press through the trials, suffering, and pain. I covenanted to fill myself with His Presence daily so that I would be sustained and able to feed others, and to share in His glory. It was marvelous.

The Wedding Dance

I was worshiping in my room when suddenly I could see gold, like transparent glass, under my feet. I looked up to see a company of people and creatures surrounding me, looking in my direction. Though I wasn't clear on where I was or what I was looking at, I could make out that some creatures were short and some tall. They were surrounding me, making a complete circle. I didn't know why they were so intently staring at me until I realized that the company of creatures and angels was not looking at me at all. They were intensely captivated by a Being of light next to me. I felt movement, and realized that I was in this Being's arms, dancing with Him.

I looked up to His face. Nobody needed to tell me who He was. In the instant that I saw His face, I knew it was Jesus, the King of Glory and Power. I had lived my whole life for that moment.

I quickly forgot about the wonder and power of the cherubim and angels that surrounded us. These angelic beings are more beautiful than anything on earth, but when compared to Him they look dim. I was instantly struck with awe by His sheer raw, untamed, and perfect beauty. Words fail to describe the beauty that radiates from Him.

The moment I saw Him it became clear to me that if He revealed Himself to everyone in this way, it would be violating the free will of man. He is so desirable that when you see Him, you no longer possess desire for anything else. Free will is marked by the ability to make a choice, but choice is not an actuality when you see Him as He is. All of your thoughts, desires, and interests completely vanish. Suddenly He is everything. Suddenly, all you want, all you are interested in, all you can focus on, is Him. Suddenly, your heart tries to involuntarily fly from your chest and into His hands in a desperate attempt to give Him all the love and worship of which He is worthy. Your very core of life, your most valued possession, is quickly thrown at His feet in hopes that He will feel just an ounce of the love that He sent coursing through your being when you simply *saw* Him. All you want is to give the love back to Him that He gave to you.

If He was revealed in this way to anyone on earth he or she would involuntarily choose Him. He is the desire of the nations. He is absolutely the fulfillment of every cry that rises up from the human heart. He is so beautiful.

I saw Him enjoying His first dance as Husband of His Bride, like a man and woman at their wedding reception. The whole procession of Heaven was in attendance. It was glorious.

I didn't want to leave. I wanted to stay in His arms and just dance forever with Him. There was nothing as beautiful as being romanced by His touch and gaze. The power He has is amazing. His power is His absolute beauty.

All those who look upon this Man will never be the same: You will be captured in an obsession that you have never known before. He is incomprehensible in His beauty. You will not be able to stop staring at Him because you will be both astounded and confounded—astounded because you have never seen anything like Him, and confounded for the same reason. He is raw power expressed through beauty.

Receive

One day during an exceptionally hard season of my life, I sat down in prayer and began to let His Presence soak me. As rest and peace came over me, I saw Jesus standing about 20 feet away from me with His hands stretched out in front of Him, reaching toward me. I knew that I shouldn't be as far away from Him as I was, and the fact that I was alerted me to where I really stood with Him. It wasn't that He didn't want to be with me, but that I was distanced from Him.

Once I realized that I had created the distance and He had not, I started walking toward Him. As I did, He parted His arms, wide open in expectation of embrace. I got close and He held me in a tight embrace. He wrapped me up in His arms and whispered in my ear, "I am so sorry for everything that has happened. I love you." I started crying, both in the vision and in real life. I fell apart. I was finally safe, finally loved, finally

understood, finally valued. I couldn't even raise my arms to hug Him back because I was so crumpled. I just received it. I needed His love badly.

We don't have to feel like we shouldn't ask Him to love us. He delights in our need for love. We can't ask Him to come love us too many times or too much.

The Garden

There is a place in the spirit that is called the garden. It is an actual place, but the only way you can visit this place is by faith. Don't be surprised; the same is true about heaven. Heaven is a place that has to be believed in to be seen. In part, the garden is the soil of your heart and spirit where the Word of God is growing like a seed. It is either watered well and is flourishing, or it is parched and dying. You can be reservoir of love, or a desert of despair. Every person has their own garden, and it is their responsibility to care for it.

So, I asked Jesus to take me to my garden. Before I knew it, I was following Him through a thick jungle. As I followed, I would watch His back disappear behind large, green plants that He pushed aside as He walked by. The thick foliage quickly gave way to a clearing. The clearing had a green canopy ceiling, hundreds of feet above it, created by the

treetops. In the clearing grew various kinds of fruit trees and flowers that do not exist on earth. I realized that this was no random plot of land, but it was somehow a garden that represented my life. This clearing was *my garden*, though it wasn't what I had expected.

Some rays of light were shining down through the trees and kept the entire garden lit, but with no more than a soft glow. It wasn't bright, yet it was not the least bit gloomy. It was private, romantic, enticing—a place for Him to get away. Safe. Abundant. Comfortable.

Jesus immediately started walking through the plants and trees, not saying much, just eating the fruits that were in this garden. It was clear that He was eating and feasting on these fruits, and that these fruits somehow represented the fruits of my life. They represented more than what I have done or become, but who I am: my personality, my characteristics, my strengths, and even my weaknesses—all of me. Most of all, these fruits represented my secret life in God, the love that I had grown for God when by myself. It was my reservoir of love that I kept for Him alone.

As He walked to and fro, Jesus turned to me and said, "I come here when I want something unique. That which is unique is my favorite." When He said this, He turned and looked at me with a smile that did not just make me feel valued, but passionately desired.

The look on His face communicated an entire book of thoughts and feelings to me. His face told me that uniqueness in and of itself makes something beautiful. In that moment I realized that being different sets something apart and gives it value. Things that are common fade in comparison to something with uniqueness. This is because in being different, something is made rare. Gold or diamonds are valuable because they are not found in abundance. When something is different, it becomes a precious distinction from that which is normal. He came to my garden to be refreshed by that which was different.

He moved about and feasted on these fruits. He was feasting on me. *He* was being strengthened by delighting in who I am. That God Himself would delight in me in such a way melted my heart.

I stood in awe of Him enjoying and replenishing Himself on who I am. As He ate, I feasted on love in an exceptional and precious way, a way that gave far more to me than what He was receiving. As He ate, I was filled.

He delights in you. Your garden is His favorite. You not only abide in His love, but He abides in yours. He calls you unique, calls you incomparably valuable, and feasts on the love that you offer to Him.

God doesn't just love you, He enjoys you. This reality breaks all shame, guilt, condemnation, and self-hatred off of a person's life. Your love is very valuable to Him.

When you take time to love God, you store up a reservoir of love for Jesus to come and partake in. Let Him eat of your love.

The Mountaintop

I sat down and closed my eyes in prayer. I felt God ask me, "Do you want to go on an adventure?"

I said yes, and suddenly Jesus and I were at the foot of a mountain. The mountain had a waterfall coming down the center of it, and Jesus started hiking toward it. We felt like brothers more than lovers in this particular escapade.

I realized that I could fast-forward or rewind the vision, or stop its play altogether and come back to it whenever I wished. It was up to me. That is the reality with God…He is not bound by the limits of continuous time. He knows how to operate within it, but also how to speed things up, slow them down, or pause things altogether. He can even go backward and look at something again.

Jesus started heading toward the waterfall. I knew that we were going to climb it, but I was also aware that in one sense we already had. I had already lived out climbing the waterfall, and had yet to live it out at the same time. The laws of time did not apply to this place. God lives outside the laws that limit us.

It became clear to me that I didn't want to skip too far ahead in this vision because I wasn't participating in the vision for the purpose of seeing what came next or the outcome of the vision. Seeing the vision wasn't the purpose. The purpose was to be with Him. If I didn't experience the vision at the same pace that He was experiencing it, there wasn't any point. It is like fast-forwarding a movie that you are watching with your spouse: You aren't watching the movie to discover the outcome of its story, but to spend time with your spouse. In this vision, Jesus had a speed, and that speed wasn't too fast or too slow, but just right so that I could get as much as possible out of what was happening. I was curious what was at the top of the rock wall that vertically intermingled with the waterfall, but decided to just enjoy my time with Jesus and let my curiosities be satisfied in due time.

I found myself walking up to the wall. He started climbing, and I followed. The rocks that were our handholds and footholds were wet, and they made for a dangerous climb. I was a bit worried and told Him so. He said, "Remember, you just realized that I am outside of time. If you were going to fall, I would know, and would either catch you or not bring you here." I realized that He was right, and it was foolish of me to even be worried a little bit if He knew what was going to happen. His omniscience killed fear in me.

As we climbed, I asked Him many questions, but He didn't answer them. I realized that I was asking questions that I didn't really want to know the answer to. The truth can be hard to stomach. He knows the difference between when we want to know the answer to something and

when we just think we want to know the answer to something. In His wisdom, He will patiently wait to give us an answer to our questions until we truly want to know what He has to say.

When we got to the top of the rock wall and climbed over the ledge, my mind lost focus. I started thinking about worldly things. Not sinful things, just things that existed in the natural realm of the world. I was gone for about three minutes, just standing at the top of the waterfall. I refocused and realized that the vision had paused and not moved on without me. What is interesting is that Jesus had realized I was gone. He wasn't upset in the least bit, but He was waiting for me with His hands on His hips.

He came up to me and put His hands on my shoulders and said, "We can't do this unless you want to." I decided that I did want to do it, refocused, and we kept walking.

We were now on the top of the mountain, in a huge, flat area. As we walked, I looked down to see that the ground was covered with very short, grass-like greenery. It was like moss but softer, greener, and cleaner.

Where we were now felt more heavenly, and I found that Jesus and I were wearing white robes. The waterfall's source was now in front of me—a river that was perfectly straight and went as far as I could see. It was crystal clear. We were on the right side of the river, and on the other side of the river were about four or five trees. They looked like large fruit trees, and doves were sitting in their branches. The whiteness of the doves was more pure and bright than anything on earth.

I asked Jesus where we were, and His answer was something I didn't expect. "This is my garden." Part of me felt bad for losing my focus in going there, but I knew He understood my weakness and wasn't upset or hurt with me. He never motivates by guilt, shame, or manipulation.

I looked at the trees and then back at Jesus, and He gestured that I should go over to the trees. In doing so I would have to cross the river, so I started in. I made my way to the other side and came out of the river feeling clean. I expected to feel more than that, but I didn't.

I walked up to the trees and realized that the doves represented the Holy Spirit, and that the fruits were the fruits of the Spirit. The fruits of Jesus are the same as the fruits of the Holy Spirit. When you feast upon Jesus, you are eating of the fruits of the Holy Spirit. So I ate.

The vision ended. I think it could have gone on as long as I had wanted, but my frailty caused my desire to be weakened. Visions are accessed through faith by desire. If you don't want it, you probably won't experience it. Most things in the Kingdom follow the same principle.

Drink and Be Filled

I entered into prayer and found myself looking at a door to a room. It was a room that was below a large house, almost hidden away like a cellar door in the basement of a house.

I opened the door and walked in to find Jesus and the Father sitting down drinking Wine. They weren't just drinking the Wine, but were clearly intoxicated. I thought to myself, "This isn't OK." I began to back out of the room, extremely uncomfortable with what I was witnessing.

Jesus looked at me, immediately sober, and calmly said, "Tyler, it is all right. It is the Holy Spirit." Trusting His words, I walked toward Jesus as He began to lose His sobriety again. The Father handed me some Wine and as I let go of my religious judgments toward God, I began to be filled by supernatural joy.

I didn't drink alone. Jesus and the Father were being so goofy, fun, and undignified. I was reminded that God was the One who created goofiness, silliness, joy, and happiness. By the end of the vision we were all drunk, hanging on each other for balance, with our heads tilted back, laughing out loud.

I have noticed that for most Christian families it is OK to be goofy in nonspiritual contexts, but that childlike goofiness is not tolerated or encouraged during prayer or worship. This is the best way to show a child that God is boring. The reality is that God doesn't compartmentalize life in the way that we do. He has fun all the time, while always being holy and reverent at the same time. Joy and holiness need to not be seen by the Church as mutually exclusive.

It was the Holy Spirit who caused the Father and Jesus to act so goofy. It was like the Holy Spirit was the Father's entertainer. Both Jesus and the Father love the Spirit. The Father loves being entertained by the Holy Spirit and the Holy Spirit loves to entertain the Father. It is a form of worship between them. It was much like the relationship between a jester and a king, yet this jester is also God and is given utmost honor from the King.

It occurred to me that God enjoys God. He delights in Himself through delighting in the other two counterparts of Himself. God doesn't just sit in Heaven bored. Nobody is as entertaining as Him, so He loves to spend time with the Son and the Spirit because they are delightful to be with!

The Holy Spirit is *the* Spirit who possesses Jesus and the Father. The Father and Jesus don't have separate spirits, but the same Spirit. In the same manner, the Spirit who gives Jesus life and who is the Father's Spirit is in *you and I*. That God would share Himself with us in this way is phenomenal.

Shaking Nations

I was in prayer, resting in the love of God. Suddenly in a vision He was in front of me in an urgent state. He came to my side and extended His hand for me to grab it. As I did, I saw that we were looking over the whole globe, as if we were seated in the heavens above the earth. Jesus told me that He was taking me higher.

When you are higher, you can see the plans of the enemy long before he attacks. You can be strategic and know where to go. When you are on earth, your ability to perceive is extremely limited to your surroundings, but when your stance is from Heaven to earth, you can perceive much more.

We looked down at the world, and I asked Jesus what I was supposed to see. He didn't answer. I noticed that He was weeping, and instinctively I knew that He was weeping about the Father's children who

have not yet been gathered into the Father's embrace. Jesus was so sad and broken.

I watched one of His tears gather in His eye and fall out, all the way to the ground. When it hit, it caused an earthquake, and I was reminded of the passage where Jesus is talking about wars and rumors of wars, earthquakes, and the like (see Matt. 24:6-7; Mark 13:7-8). I knew what He was trying to give me was a heart of brokenness for those who do not know Him: a passion for souls. But though I saw Him cry, I did not cry. I desire to be moved by love to the same degree He is. I need to weep as He weeps. I need my heart torn and changed into His. I have never seen Jesus upset, anxious, or concerned, except in this vision. He was deeply troubled.

Jesus isn't worried about the devil; He already beat him on the cross. He isn't worried about cancer; He destroyed its power when He died. He doesn't get concerned about anything except one thing: that Christians aren't helping people who don't know Him to be born again. He is distressed about all the people in the world who will go to hell if we don't tell them about Him. He is distressed not over unbelievers, but over believers because they aren't getting the unbelievers saved. He isn't worried about anything or anyone but us. He has done all that He can do to save the world, even gave Himself over to death. He can't make us win souls and heal hearts and bodies. He won't force us to do anything. He has done all that He can do and now He is trusting us to love Him enough to save others.

Three days after this vision, I picked up a newspaper to find that an earthquake took place in the exact place where I saw the tear from Jesus' eye fall.

The Provision Room

I was alone in prayer when I found myself standing in front of a door. Jesus said, "This is where you wanted to come, right?" He took out a key and unlocked the door. Most doors in Heaven aren't locked, but this one was.

We walked through the door to see gigantic mounds of gold coins and precious stones. The piles were so high that they could be compared to skyscrapers. The room we had walked into was specifically made to house monetary items such as gold.

I went in and took about five gold coins and a jewel. I didn't want to take more than that. I knew I could come back when I needed more. I felt like I shouldn't take more, but I don't know why.

Jesus seemed a bit disappointed. He said, "Is that all you are going to take? You can take as little as you wish, but know that Daddy has more than enough and that He trusts you with taking more if you want to."

I thought about what He said for a second, and as a spirit of poverty died in me, I turned around and went back for more. I filled a book bag full of the precious coins and stones, and looked across the room in hopes of spotting Daddy so that I could thank Him.

On the wall, high above the floor, was a window that looked out over the gold and jewels. Daddy was standing in that window watching over His finances. I suddenly jumped in His direction to meet Him. This wasn't logical, because even if I somehow jumped all the way over to Him, there was still a window that I would run into. However, in the vision the window disappeared, and He caught me in His arms.

In visions and encounters a person is functioning in a realm that is not limited by the natural laws that the earth is limited by. When one looks across distances, he instinctively knows exactly how far it is. When a person attempts to communicate, it can happen through his thoughts just as clearly as through the use of his mouth. When one walks from one place to another, he can travel as quickly or as slowly as he likes in getting there, because in heavenly realms a person travels by thought. In Heaven, if a person wants to visit a place, he simply thinks of it, and faith literally takes him there. Every natural law in Heaven swiftly gives way to an ounce of faith. If a window is in one's way, it will be removed with a simple act of faith.

As the window vanished, He caught me, and I was transformed into a little boy. I thanked Him for the provision, then swung myself onto His back and asked Him to give me a piggyback ride. He laughed at my request, then spun me around in the room on His back.

Once the ride was over, He cradled me in His arms with joy like a Father holds a newly born baby. He told me that He loved me very much, and in that instant I was grown again, standing next to Him as the vision ceased.

Glory

I was praying in my room when I saw myself kneeling before Jesus as a knight would kneel before a king.

He took something that looked like a large piece of cloth and draped it over me as He said, "Receive My glory." This made me very uncomfortable. I said, "Lord, You are the only One who is supposed to have glory." He said, "I understand. But in order to walk in My glory, you must first possess it."

I had never thought about glory in such a way. Glory is a substance more than it is the worship that comes from man. I despise, even hate, man's worship of anything but God. The worship of one man by another is poison to the mind and heart of the one who receives it. While I hate

man's worship, I do want the substance that God enthrones Himself in to rest upon my life. Let us not confuse the two.

The Bible says that His Glory will cover the earth like the water covers the sea (see Hab. 2:14). I meditated on that verse and realized that the weight of water at the bottom of the ocean is amazing. One thing that the verse is saying is that His Glory will come with such weight and distribution across the earth that we will be pinned down and drowned in this heavenly substance called glory. Glory is a substance, like faith.

The Wedding Procession

I was in prayer and saw Jesus and me standing up on a stage before the Father. We stood before Him as Bride and Groom, and He was like a minister who was about to marry the two of us. God the Father will preside at the greatest wedding of all of history.

The Father spoke briefly, and then told Jesus He could kiss the Bride. He lifted my veil and told me, "This is the veil I tore when I died. This veil hindered us from intimacy, but now I can show you My affection." Then He gently kissed me.

The veil is the object that keeps us from seeing Him clearly and keeps Him from freely showing His affection to us and us to Him. The veil keeps us from entering into deeper places of love with God. Kisses metaphorically represent intimacy with Jesus, but they can only happen once the veil has been lifted or torn. I always believed that the only veil

that Jesus tore when He died was the one in the temple, but Song of Songs speaks of a different veil (see 4:1,3; 6:7). Paul also mentions a veil in Second Corinthians 3:14. Because of the finished work of the Cross, both veils are now lifted, making way for a reality that generations past wished for: intimacy with God Himself.

When we receive Jesus in His death for us, the veil is lifted and we immediately enter into marital love with Jesus. Intimacy with Jesus is suddenly made available to us. His kisses become a reality, not just something we wish for. If we feel that we aren't experiencing intimacy with God, it isn't because He doesn't want it for us, or that He hasn't done everything for us to have it. Everything we need was finished at the Cross. The door is open on His end. If He feels far away, it cannot be truth, for He told us that He would never leave us or forsake us because He is bound by the contract of marriage. We never need to fear that He will leave us, because He promised to always be near.

We will consummate our marriage to the King of Kings on our honeymoon, one that will last millions of years (Heaven). This divinely epic honeymoon will never stop.

Once Jesus had kissed His Bride, the ceremony was over. Unlike our ceremonies today, the Father led everyone out, not the Bride and Bridegroom. As He went, a Spirit of joy came on Him and He began to dance. He even did cartwheels down the aisle. He was overwhelmingly ecstatic about the fact that His Son was finally married. We followed Him in joy as the entire company of people and angels followed us. It was the most delightful celebration that I have ever witnessed.

Miracles Observed Firsthand

Below is a list of miracles that I had the honor of seeing take place firsthand. Many of the miracles mentioned below are not in story form like the rest of the miracles in this book because many have no story. Sometimes we prayed and the person was instantly made well, with very little interaction between the person and myself. Hence, they are below in a short, succinct form.

The majority of the following miracles took place in a three-year period. The purpose of adding them at the end of the book in this fashion is for the sake of showing the reader what can happen in a three-year period. If they believe that God is good and wants to make others better, they will find themselves making their own list of miracles that God did through them.

Anyone can work miracles. All you need is love and the Holy Spirit. These miracles did not come about through the use of any type of ministerial platform that is unattainable to the average Christian. I was not in full-time ministry, being paid to do the work of the Kingdom. I was working a normal job. These miracles took place during the walking out of everyday life. God uses simple people that don't have any special credentials. "Just believe."

HanMarie's back

Three women in a small church in Edernet

Mother of the girls who sold eggs

A crippled woman in Hovsgol

A baby in Beirut with yellow fever

Rachel's back at Walmart

A woman who grew feminine parts that had been surgically removed

Man's knee at Walmart

A woman with MS in Healing Rooms

Girl's elbow and shoulder in Walmart with Jamin

Matt's shoulder in Healing Rooms

Man with emphysema in Healing Rooms

Deaf man in Healing Rooms

Danny's knees at exit 154

Jared's knee in parking lot

Hispanic man growing reproductive organ in parking lot

Woman's back and hip in grocery store

Man's back just walking by us

Ashley's (pagan witch) chest cold

Woman's arthritic foot at Bethel

Miracles Observed Firsthand

Man's arthritic shoulders at Bethel

Woman's arthritic knees at Bethel

Dorothy's progressive healing in her back
after forgiving her father

Christopher's emphysema, new kneecap,
better vision

Hispanic girl's legs in Mexico

Hispanic man's hips in Mexico

Boy with scoliosis in Mexico

Woman's leg at Healing Rooms

Woman's leg and hip at Healing Rooms

Two-year-old with terminal brain
problems

William in Aberdeen—bolts in foot and
ankle disappeared

Girl's ear opened up in Aberdeen

Foot pain for two men in Aberdeen

Donna's diabetes and allergies gone

Homeless man's back in San Francisco

Denise's daughter's incredible back pain

Cancerous cysts in man's throat gone

Girl with migraine in the streets of
Spokane

Man's shoulders in Healing Rooms

Elderly woman with leg and back problems in Healing Rooms

Older man wrongly accused of crime, with leg and back problems

Young woman blind from birth

Woman with fibromyalgia in Healing Rooms

Leg that grew out in Eastern Washington

Multiple sclerosis healed in Oregon

Man's knee at car auction

Stephan's feet at Andrew's house

Woman's deaf ear opened in California

Man's degenerative disks of 30 years

Cracked teeth made whole

Cancerous tumor disappears on MRI

About the Author

Tyler and his wife, Christine, live in Washington when they are not in the nations spreading a spirit of revival and fire. They regularly preach at churches and conferences and are deeply in love with Jesus.

www.oneglance.org
www.deadraisingteam.com

Contact us at:

oneglanceministies@gmail.com

For all critical, discouraging, accusatory, religious, and altogether unhelpful e-mails, please write to:

wenevercheckthisemail@gmail.com

Also Available from One Glance Ministries…

One Glance Ministries desires that the Body of Christ be trained and equipped to do the work of the ministry. Our hope is that through the teachings found here, you will be filled with fire from Heaven, and that others will come to the knowledge of God's goodness through YOU. If you cannot afford something we are selling and are hungry for some spiritual food, contact us and we will make sure you get what you need. Blessings!

www.oneglance.org
Short Reads:

Loved by Love (71 pages)

This book is a modern-day rendering of The Song of Songs into a prayerful conversation of intimacy between you and Jesus. The Song of Songs is one of the most profound books in the Bible. There is no book in the Bible that more accurately captures the emotions of God's heart toward people as The Song of Songs. There is an enormous release of revelation, confidence, and power that spills forth into the life of the believer who receives from the love that is captured in the verses of this book.

The Two Imperatives for Every Believer (27 pages)

This book is a succinct overview of two imperative topics: righteousness and the goodness of God.

A misunderstanding of righteousness has resulted in much of the Body of Christ believing that their righteousness is determined by their

actions rather than by faith. When we realize righteousness is a gift we receive through faith rather than something we earn, an earth-shattering transformation takes place in our lives. We begin to live out of freedom rather than fear, and our hearts come alive to the love and goodness of God.

The goodness of God is the biggest fight that a Christian faces in life. The goodness of God is the key to the power of God and the secret to unlock the freedom that comes from being wholly loved. If a person can truly believe that God is good and have a way of reading the Bible that is congruent to that belief, nothing will be impossible for him or her. For this person, raising the dead, killing giants, saving whole nations in a day, and even literal flying are nothing more than a "walk in the park."

Messages available on CD or MP3 download:

The Power of the Tongue

Seated in Heavenly Places of Intimacy

The Fire of Love and Revival

Prophetic Evangelism Training

Ministering in Your Local Community

He That Is Within Is Greater

The Painful Joy of Following Jesus

Desire and Desperation

He Loves Your Love

The Dead Raising Team

And More…

Messages available on DVD:

The Power of the Tongue

Victorious

Shirts:

We sell shirts with witty, nonreligious remarks on them. Wear them to church and you may offend people, but wear them to your local Walmart and people may get saved, healed, and delivered!

All items can be found at:
www.oneglance.org

Additional copies of this book and other book titles from DESTINY IMAGE are available at your local bookstore.

Call toll-free: 1-800-722-6774.

Send a request for a catalog to:

Destiny Image® Publishers, Inc.

P.O. Box 310
Shippensburg, PA 17257-0310

"Speaking to the Purposes of God for This Generation and for the Generations to Come."

For a complete list of our titles, visit us at www.destinyimage.com.